"Sons of Darkness, Sons of Light"

A True Crime Story

by Marilyn Miller

ISBN 1-893693-09-0

Published by
SWEET DREAMS PUBLISHING COMPANY
P.O. BOX 850 ~ MANY, LA 71449
Ph. (318) 256-3495 FAX (318) 256-9151
www.sweetdreamspub.com

PRINTED 2000 IN THE UNITED STATES OF AMERICA

MHS'TO

To Betty Rose -
We grew up together
and are still going strong!
Love Ya!
Marilyn
Nov. 7, 2000

"Ye are all the children of light;
And the children of the day.
Ye are not of the night,
Nor of darkness..."

I Thessalonians 5:5

FOREWARD

In July of 1989 I was working as executive editor of the Minden Press-Herald, a daily newspaper covering news and events in Minden and south Webster Parish. It was during this time that I received the following letter:

Dear Editor,

I am trying to locate some relatives that still may be in your area. If you would print this, maybe someone would see it that could help me. My great-grandfather, Robert Maier, lived around Hardie, Louisiana around 1918, along with Westley, his son. A daughter, Maude, married John Nelson Reeves. They were murdered Christmas Eve 1916 along with three children. The only child that I know survived was Cody. There may have been more.

Another daughter, Annie, married Howard Paul. Their children were John Howard Paul and Annie May Paul. These may still be living or at least some of their children may be, in your area.

This is all the information I have. I know it has been a long time, but maybe someone would have knowledge of where these people may be found. Please write if you have information, or call.

Sincerely,

Mrs. Carolyn Brown

Hendersonville, North Carolina

As was our custom at the *Press-Herald*, we printed the letter. I then put it out of my mind.

The evening after the letter was printed, I received a phone call from my father. Now I couldn't remember my father ever having picked up a phone to call and chat. Phones were for emergencies and important messages only (and, of course, making fishing and hunting plans.) I knew he wasn't calling to make a fishing date, so I was curious.

"Your grandfather was a witness at that trial," he said.

I wondered about his sanity.

"What trial, Daddy?"

"That trial - that Reeves trial. That letter that was in the paper…the Reeves woman who was killed. Your grandfather was a witness at that trial."

And so it began…my investigation into a murder that started out as a curiosity, blossomed into a passion, and culminated with this book.

It doesn't take everyone ten years to write a book, even when extensive research is required. This one did. I suspended my writing when I started a new job in late 1990, and didn't really begin again in earnest until 1996 - the year my father was diagnosed with terminal cancer. I wanted so badly to complete the manuscript before he died.

But I didn't, and I regret it. He died in December of 1996 without even reading a draft. This book is dedicated to him.

I worked in the newspaper business for 17 years, and if there was one lesson I learned, it's that you can't make everyone happy - no matter what you are writing about. I'm sure this book will make some people unhappy.

"Why reopen old wounds from the past?" they'll ask. "Why not let the past remain in the past?"

I considered changing some names to protect innocent family members, but that would only lessen the integrity of the work. And, we are all innocent. We are not responsible for the actions of our ancestors...nor will our offspring be responsible for what we do today. And all criminals, hardened or petty, come from families - good families.

Why bring up the past?

Because this story needs to be told.

This story is not just about murder, it's about equal justice and human fairness. This story is not about politics - it's about the *consequences* of politics and power -- what happens when people give up or lose the battle of wills to the politicians. It's about good and evil. It's about darkness...and light.

I regret that as I complete this book, I still don't have all the answers. After years of research and interviews, I still can't say, without a doubt, that justice was done.

We'll probably never know.

Acknowledgements

I would like to extend many thanks to the Webster Parish Clerk of Court's Office, and specifically Clerk of Court Winnie Brinkley and Deputy Clerk Marcella Shaw; the Webster Parish Library staff, John Agan, Karyn Noles Bewley, Judy O. Williams, Steve Fomby, Michelle Finley, the Shreve Memorial Library staff, the Shreveport Times, the Shreveport Journal, the Minden Press-Herald, Robert Gentry, the Louisiana State Archives, the late Mr. John T. Campbell, the late Mr. Annon Pevy; to my many friends, family members, and co-workers, who believed in me -- and most especially, to my late father, Mr. W. S. Miller, to whom this book is dedicated. His phone call started this literary journey.

Prologue

Monday, December 25, 1916
Grove, Louisiana

Only the occasional barking of a dog interrupts the post-midnight calm. In the distance, the rising and falling torrent of voices bantering over a low-stakes crap game can no longer be heard -- a symptom of those dead hours between midnight and dawn.

Smoke drifts soundlessly from the chimneys of isolated rooftops dotting the countryside of bare, meandering fields and shivering pine trees.

In the summertime, mile after mile of blossoming cotton plants, their billowing white bolls gleaming in the humid Louisiana sun, would fill the landscape. But not on the 25th day of December -- not even in the South.

The sound of feet shuffling heavily over gnarled roots and dried mud of the neglected farm road intrudes upon the natural night sounds. Five mysterious figures materialize without warning, like haunting apparitions in a familiar fairy tale. They talk in shrouded whispers...their words turning to fog in the cold night air.

Just as suddenly as they appear, the men leave the road...striking off across a small field of row crops...past withered remnants of once-proud corn stalks standing guard over decaying frost-laden vines, which crackle and crunch beneath their feet.

From somewhere nearby, a horse snorts, adding to the nocturnal cacophony as the silhouettes huddle together under a copse of trees shading a lone cabin.

The little house is dark and unassumingly peaceful...barely defined against the winter night blackness by a glint of light radiating from a rear window and pearl-gray smoke ghosting lazily from the chimney.

One of the men, his brooding features hidden beneath the brim of his sweat-stained, tattered fedora, gestures towards the porch. His sudden movements send a splash of light heavenward as moonlight finds the cold metal of the object he grips in his hand.

An ax.

PART I

"I wish Pa didn't snore so loud. Santa Claus might not stop here if'n he hears Pa snorin' so loud."

Seven-year-old Cody Reeves burrowed deeper into the pile of clean clothes his mother had thrown on the bed -- and promptly forgot. She had more important things on her mind than folding clothes. It was Christmas Eve.

Cody's brothers, nine-year-old David, five-year-old Woodrow, and 15-month-old Alto were sleeping on pallets nearer the fireplace to stay warm. They'd gone to bed around 11:30, but Cody was too excited to sleep.

Normally, he would have joined his brothers on the floor. But he figured Santa would be using the chimney tonight, and he wasn't too keen on meeting the fat whiskered drover face-to-face, much as he admired him and all. He really marveled over the way Santa could keep from getting' all burned up in the fire...

"David says there ain't no Santa Claus," Cody thought, the weight of sleep lying heavily on his flickering eyelids. "Maybe he knows, 'cause he's older'n me. Or maybe he just don't wanta believe there's a Santa Claus 'cause if he don't come by our house, he won't have to blame Pa."

Pa was mean sometimes...

Cody didn't know why his father was mean, but he knew he got even meaner when he drank. And he had been drinking that night. He always snored loud when he passed out drunk -- and he was really sawin' some logs.

Cody hoped Santa wouldn't skip their house 'cause Pa was mean and snored loud.

He snuggled deeper into his cocoon of quilts and clothes, leaving only his nose exposed to the crisp winter air in the room.

Everyone but Mama had already gone to bed. He could see a light shining in the kitchen and knew she was in there, probably choppin' and cuttin' and getting' everything ready for Christmas dinner. He hoped she remembered to put out milk and cookies for Santa.

2

If Mama put out milk and cookies, that meant she believed in Santa Claus. And she was older 'n David....a lots older.

He remembered David sayin' somethin' 'bout Mama bein' 30 years old. That was old. But Pa, he was even older 'n Mama...fact, he was twiced as old as Mama. At least that's what he'd heard Mr. Johnson say t'other day. And everbody called 'im 'old man.' Wonder if'n he's as old as Santa Claus.

Nobody liked Pa much. But they'd sure come 'round when there was card playin' and drinkin' going on. Pa'd usually end up in a fight. Cody had once heard somebody say that his Pa was too mean to die.

He wondered if Santa Claus would bring something to his Pa if'n he was too mean to die.

He could barely keep his eyes open now. The heavy covers and clothes were doing the job...warming him up.

He thought about an argument between he and David earlier. His older brother had accused him of being scared of Santa Claus. Said that's why he wouldn't sleep on the floor near the fireplace.

He'd flat denied it to David...but kinda admitted it to himself.

Mama, sensing this, had assured him that Santa would come, even if he was a scaredy cat. Maybe Santa'd bring him that slingshot. David wanted a shotgun so's he could shoot rabbits and squirrels. Pa had a gun -- he'd seen it. But it weren't no shotgun, he could hold it in his hand. He'd seen his Pa point it at a fella one time when he was real mad.

Just for a moment, Cody considered slipping out of bed and taking a peek at what his mother was doing. Earlier that night he'd seen her sneak some packages out of the storeroom...maybe she was wrappin' him a present at this very moment!

But the warm covers won out. Just the thought of having to get warm all over again made him snuggle deeper into his hiding place.

"I'll just close my eyes for a little while," he thought. "Just for a little while."

Monday, January 29, 1917
Webster Parish Courthouse
Minden, Louisiana

"Mr. Johnson, you are a resident of Grove, Louisiana, are you not?"

Harmon C. Drew, the young district attorney for Bossier and Webster Parishes, crossed his arms over the beginnings of a barreled chest and walked confidently toward the witness. He stopped just in front of the man he was questioning, leaning in toward him, his weight shifting forward to the balls of his feet.

Spectators who were crammed into the normally spacious main courtroom of the Webster Parish Courthouse strained forward, afraid that Drew's broad-shouldered, suspender-clad bulk might inhibit them from hearing what the witness had to say.

"You live about a quarter of a mile from the home of John Nelson Reeves, isn't that right?"

"Yes, sir, I sure do."

The witness, Jewell Johnson, sat back and pulled at the collar of his starched "Sunday" shirt. He'd be glad when this trial was over and he could get back to his farm...and more comfortable clothes.

"Mr. Johnson, would you describe for this court the events that took place in your life on the morning of December 25, 1916?" Drew stepped back, intent on giving the jury a clear view of the witness. The appreciative spectators visibly relaxed.

"Yes, sir," Johnson answered, tugging at the irritating collar again. He'd told this story at least a thousand times. He would always remember that Christmas morning.

Always.

****

It was barely daylight...too damn early for someone to be banging on his door. He opened it to find his neighbor, Will Smith, looking like a cat that's come face to face with its Maker.

"Jewel, looks like we got a problem" Smith blurted out. "J. W. got me outta bed this morning -- said one of the Reeves boys was holler'n and carryin' on, and when he checked it out, the boy had blood all over him. J.W. asked the boy how he got so bloody, and the youngun told him everybody'd been killed over to his house. Said he tried to wake his brother up and that's where the blood

4

come from. Grady and me went on over there. There was blood all in the yard and up on the porch all right. We didn't go in the house though...you know how crazy old man Reeves is...thought I might better get some help."

Smith finally paused to take a breath.

Jewell stepped back into the house and tossed on an old flannel shirt.

"Come on," he said, leaping from the porch and heading in the direction of the Reeves cabin.

"I was kinda worried about going over to the Reeves place alone, Jewel," Smith prattled on, hurrying to keep up. "You know the old man -- he mighta been on a drunk -- coulda killed some of the family himself. Grady and me thought we might need some help if he was still drunk. J.W. agreed. That's why we come to get you."

As they drew close to the house, Jewell made out the silhouetted forms of J.W. Braselton, his son Grady, and Cody Reeves. They were hanging back near the road. Johnson nodded a mute greeting and walked into the yard, where the bloody artifacts of an unnaturally violent night greeted him through the December morning mist.

He leaned over and poked at a blood-stained rag resting in the yard. Deliberately, he climbed the steps to the porch, all the while keeping an eye on the door of the cabin. He didn't want to be surprised by a booze-crazed, gun-wielding homeowner.

A bucket of crimson-colored water caught his eye. Water turned that color when you soaked freshly-butchered deer, squirrel or rabbit parts in it. Quarter-sized splotches of dried blood polka-dotted the porch planks. But it was the sight of a bloody hand imprint on the doorframe that unsettled Johnson most. He backed lightly down the steps, rejoining the others.

"J. W., why don't you and Grady take the boy on back to your house and keep him there. Then I want you to fetch the sheriff."

Will Smith looked woefully at Johnson as he talked, wishing he'd been the one sent to safety. Instead, after the Braseltons herded Cody off down the road, Johnson motioned for Smith to follow him back up to the porch. He crept closer to the door.

"John, you in there?" he yelled, feeling spooked. He rapped again. "Mrs. Reeves...hello...anybody there?"

He wondered just for a brief second if Reeves might be lying in wait, ready to shoot him if he entered the house.

"We might ought to wait for the sheriff," Smith whispered, echoing Jewell Johnson's unspoken fears.

He started to back away, then stopped.

"Did you hear that?" He half-whispered the question to Smith, who was already retreating from the porch.

"I didn't hear nuthin'," Smith answered, backing away.

Then he heard it again. A moan. A child's whimper...

"I'm going in," Johnson said, giving the door a reluctant shove. Smith didn't budge.

It was semi-dark in the small cabin. He paused to allow his eyes to adjust, wishing suddenly for something, anything resembling a weapon. He couldn't quite place a peculiar, pungent smell...

Without venturing any further into the room, he fumbled in his pants pocket for a match. Finding one, he pulled it out with slightly trembling fingers, struck it on the leg of his pants, and awkwardly held it above his head.

The eerie, dancing cast-off glow of the match fire afforded just enough light for Jewell Johnson to witness the most gruesome picture of his life.

In the chilly, tomblike room a little boy lie on a pallet in front of a waning fire, curled up in a fetal position, bathed in blood, either unconscious, or dead. Johnson leaned over to get a closer look, afraid to touch the child, afraid of touching death. A low moan bubbled from the boy's lips at exactly the same time Johnson's match played out. A split-second wave of hysteria pulsed through him and he plunged his hand deep into his pocket for another one.

The child was still alive.

What monster could have attacked a little one so brutally? Certainly not his own father.

"Son, can you hear me?" Johnson whispered, leaning close with the match. "Who did this to you? Can you hear me?"

Getting no answer, he straightened up and struck another match.

Old man Reeves lie dead in his bed...his head split clean in two, mouth sagging open, eyes staring vacantly, crimson oozing from every crevice. Blood and pieces of flesh decorated the walls, dripping and oozing down to the floor, where it stuck to Johnson's shoes when he leaned over to get a closer look. Parts of Reeves' brain had splattered out upon his arm.

Johnson straightened up and involuntarily shivered. Daylight was beginning to filter into the musty, dank cabin. He entered the next room, a combination kitchen/dining room.

A young boy, his head, face and chest a pulpy, red stew, sat half erect on the floor. Next to him, squirming around in his own blood as it pooled and commingled with his brother's, was an infant. As the baby would try to crawl away, the older boy would reach out and pull him back.

Seeing Johnson, the youth tried to sit up and hold the baby to him.

"Please help my brother...please help him," the young man's appeal to Johnson was so faint he had to strain to hear him.

"We're gonna help you, son...just keep still now. Help is on the way...What happened? Who did this to you? Where's your mama?"

"Mama? I don't know...would you help Alto...don't let him die...please..."

Johnson patted the boy on the leg reassuringly and went to get Smith and anyone else who could help.

One by one they removed the children to the Braselton's, who had been instructed to place a call to the sheriff's office. They left Reeves were he was, and went in search of his wife. Jewell Johnson hoped that she was alive and hiding somewhere, so she could tell them what happened.

They found her outside, about 40 or 50 feet away from the main house. She was lying face down, like she'd been running away. A bloody, gaping hole in the back of her head was testimony to the way she died.

Johnson remembered how cold she was to the touch.

And that she was barefooted.

****

Johnson stopped talking.

The room had grown quiet. The hands of a wall clock irreverently ticked off the seconds.

7

Harmon Drew cleared his throat.

"Did you notice anything unusual in the house," he began, "Any furniture broken...or any sign of a weapon...Anything like that?"

"Well sir, we poked around some more outside...but we didn't find nothin' there...no sign of any weapon or nothing. But when we went back on the porch, we noticed that an old tool box had been forced open. I seem to remember that Reeves kept his change in a tool chest that he kept in a storeroom in the house. Well, it was broken open...we figured somebody robbed old man Reeves...and killed everybody...maybe they didn't want no witnesses...maybe they was just mean."

"Thank you, Mr. Johnson."

Turning back toward the spectators, the prosecutor hesitated.

"Just one more thing Mr. Johnson. At any time did Cody Reeves tell you how he managed to escape being attacked like the other members of his family?"

"Well, sir, I can only speculate on that by what he told me...said he was asleep in a pile of wash...I think they just didn't see him."

The prosecutor, a father himself, turned and allowed his gaze to rest on a small boy in the audience. His pause was perfectly timed.

"Thank you, Mr. Johnson."

****

Court-appointed defense attorney D. Webster Stewart was by far the oldest living member of the Webster Parish Bar Association. He made no effort to examine Jewell Johnson, apparently satisfied with his testimony.

So Drew wasted no time in calling his next witness, A. Hutchinson Phillips.

Unlike Johnson, Webster Parish Sheriff Hutch Phillips looked comfortable on the witness stand. In difference to propriety, he had taken off his Stetson and balanced it on one knee. To some, he looked almost naked. Few people ever saw him without it.

He relaxed and surveyed the courtroom. It was filled to overflowing. The sight of so many of the area's farmers and merchants in their "Sunday starched best" amused him. Even a few

8

ladies had managed to ease their way into what he called the "arena of the law." No Negroes, though.

He decided that the dozen or so special deputies he'd posted throughout the room looked pretty intimidating with their serious faces and their big guns. Some had managed to take their jobs too seriously, but that went with the territory.

At his instruction, everyone entering the courtroom had been searched. They had turned up a few pocket knives -- one as big as a meat cleaver. That had given them pause for thought.

In the interest of security, District Judge John N. Sandlin had ordered the sheriff to appoint the team of special deputies to help "police" the courthouse during the trial. These men, though temporary, were reliable. They were all good men. W.T. Barnett, W.H. Webb, W.G. Fields, brothers Charles and Ben Beaird, John O'Rear, J.H. Maddry, Charles L. Whitmarsh, Milam Miller, T.F. Greene, John C. Tillman, and Dan Watts. All were stationed around the room and along the corridors, and outside. No one got by without inspection.

****

Truth of the matter was, Judge Sandlin's concerns for security were not without merit.

It had been very early on a Sunday morning - September 9, 1894 - when an angry mob of 21 men had forced their way into the Webster Parish Jail bent on lynching outlaw Link Waggoner.

John Sandlin, an idealistic 22-year-old, had been one of the few men with courage enough to stand up to the mob.

He had run to the nearby Presbyterian Church and begun to ring the bell and fire his pistol into the air to draw attention. However, his efforts had been thwarted and he'd been forced at gunpoint to hide under the church steps until Waggoner was dead.

Judge John Sandlin was determined that this would never happen again.

****

"Sheriff Phillips, you were called upon to investigate an incident that took place in Grove, Louisiana on December 25, 1916 were you not?"

Harmon Drew, hands resting on his hips, nodded as the sheriff answered in the affirmative, and threw out the next question.

"Just for the court's information, sir, where is Grove?"

9

Sheriff Phillips looked at the man he respected and admired. He had always appreciated Drew's undaunted commitment to the law -- and his wit. When the sheriff attended his swearing in as district attorney for the Second Judicial District only two months earlier, Drew had promised the people that he was going to blot out bootlegging.

This murder was certainly a hell of a case for a first-year DA. But Drew was up to the challenge. It was, quite simply, in his blood.

"Well, sir, for the record," Phillips answered, "Minden is the parish seat for Webster, and Grove is about, oh, 'bout five miles north of Minden...Got a post office there...serves a good many families in the Grove, Evergreen, and Germantown communities, mostly cotton farmers...It's not a real big place...pretty spread out."

"And you got a call to go to Grove early Christmas morning?"

"Yes sir. Got a call from one of my deputies...said we ought to go check out the report of a murder...Said the neighbors of a John Nelson Reeves had called and reported some killings...So I took Deputy Watts and we drove up there. That was about eight o'clock."

"And what did you find when you arrived, Sheriff Phillips?"

"When we got there, we found the first body outside the house. Neighbors helped us identify her as Maud Reeves. She was fully clothed -- with the exception of her shoes. She was lying face down, and it appeared that she had been shot or bludgeoned in the back of the head. Anyway, her skull was crushed...and her body had been pretty badly cut up. She was lying about 40 to 50 feet from the back door -- near a smokehouse of sorts. It looked like she had been running from the house. At that point, I told one of the neighbors to fetch Doc Tompkins, the coroner, and we entered the house."

Sheriff Phillips drew a deep breath.

"Continue, sir," Drew pressed.

"Well, I've been a peace officer for a long time and I've seen a lot of things...but I've never seen anything like what we found in that house. And that's after the children had been

10

removed. I can't imagine how Mr. Johnson must have felt...being the first person on the scene."

The entire gallery of spectators leaned forward as the sheriff talked. No one wanted to miss a word.

"There was blood everywhere. We found Mr. Reeves in his bed. His head had been bashed open and he had deep wounds over most of his upper body. I guessed at that point that the murder weapon was either an ax or a hatchet. Anyway, from the position of the body and all, I'd say he died instantly."

"What about the children, Sheriff? Did you get a chance to question them?" Drew asked.

"I looked in on the boys...but they'd lost so much blood...they were too far gone to answer any questions. The older boy's skull was fractured and he appeared to have some pretty deep wounds on his face, neck and chest. The baby was badly cut up, too. Both of them were still soaked in blood when we got there...and they'd been bleedin' for some time. The middle boy had been hacked up pretty good. The loss of blood was our most serious concern. We hoped we could save 'em, so my deputies rushed 'em back to Minden and put 'em on the train to Shreveport so they could be treated at Charity Hospital. Doc Tompkins motored one of the boys over in his own car."

"Did you talk to the neighbors about the family, Sheriff Phillips?"

"Yes, sir. Through the neighbors we determined that Mr. Reeves was apparently in his late 60s, and his wife was 30. She was the former Maud Myers from Pollock. They hadn't lived in the parish long...probably less than a year, but they'd been married about 12 years...and had the four kids. The old man has several grown children by a previous marriage -- some of 'em live around here. I think one grown boy lives in Hortman."

The sheriff's voice trailed off, giving Drew the chance to pose another question.

"Sheriff Phillips, I know you can't tell us exactly when this heinous crime took place. But by evidence you found at the scene, can you speculate on the time of the attacks?"

"Well, I would say everything took place well after midnight. The kitchen bore signs of food preparation -- Mrs. Reeves must have been planning a big Christmas dinner. But she didn't have any shoes on when we found her, and that would indicate that she was either getting ready for bed, or that she was trying not to make any noise that would wake up the children. In fact, I'd say the assailants surprised her while she was laying out the Christmas presents. She apparently ran out of the house to escape, and they ran her down."

For a second the sheriff appeared lost in thought. His mind returned to a picture of a kitchen table filled with Christmas toys. He could picture the happy mother carefully laying them out...something for each child. Everything in that house seemed to be covered in blood...except for those gifts on that table.

Drew cleared his throat, bringing the sheriff back to the present.

"Yes, I'd say it was well after midnight, probably closer to 2 or 3 o'clock. We found three sets of tracks leading from the house. With that many people involved, you'd think somebody would have noticed some activity around the place if it had been any earlier. So I'd speculate that the attack happened way up in the morning...after all the Christmas Eve celebrating died down."

"Sheriff Phillips, why do you think the Reeves were murdered?"

"Objection, your honor. The distinguished counselor is leading the witness to draw a conclusion," Webster Stewart drawled and gently gestured towards the judge.

Drew was slightly startled, the first objection by the defense attorney catching him off-guard. Up to this point, Stewart had been happy to let Drew run the show.

"Your honor, this goes to motive. And we're not asking the witness to draw any conclusions...just to speculate on any obvious reasons for the murders based on evidence found at the crime scene," Drew retorted.

Judge Sandlin looked sternly towards the defense attorney, appearing anything but happy. He knew the direction this case was going, and it was a shame there was no way it could be fair. The case had turned his courtroom into a circus and he resented it. But there wasn't much he could do about it.

"You may answer the question, Sheriff, but don't draw any conclusions about guilt or innocence that might sway the jury one way or the other."

"Continue, Sheriff."

"Well, Reeves was not a man who much believed in banks - that was a well-known fact." He said this looking first at Stewart and then the judge. "He was not a well-respected man...was known to be pretty mean. He had no regular occupation. In fact, he was known to bootleg and gamble to make a living -- and illegal fishin' wasn't beneath him either. On the other hand, he was known to brag a lot about the money he kept in a chest on his place. In fact, the neighbors said he had recently bragged about having $4,000 stashed in a tool chest at his place that he would 'defend with hot lead' if he had to. Since the tool chest had been forced open...and it was empty...I'd have to guess that the assailants planned to rob the old man. How it turned into butchery...I certainly can't say."

"Have you recovered any money?" Drew asked.

"No, sir, and there's nothing to prove that the old man really had the money...just some folks who said his wife mighta inherited a small sum a short time ago."

Both Drew and Stewart seemed satisfied with the sheriff's answer.

So Drew maneuvered the testimony into a new direction.

"Tell us about your investigation...after you discovered the bodies...and sent the children to the hospital...what happened next, Sheriff Phillips?"

Deputy Calhoun Garland was tired. It was after 9 o'clock and he'd been on his feet since being summoned to Grove by Sheriff Phillips early that morning -- just about the time he was preparing to enjoy a hearty Christmas breakfast with his family.

Who wants to go and murder a whole family on Christmas day anyway? Ain't it bad enough to kill someone -- kids at that? And you gotta go and do it on Christmas to boot?

They'd learned just a few hours ago that two of the Reeves children had died at the hospital. That left only the baby...and his chances weren't good.

Yep, he thought, hanging ain't gonna be good enough for whoever done this -- the bastards.

Calhoun had never seen anything like what he had witnessed that morning. He'd be willing to bet that the floor of the Reeves house was shoe sole deep in sticky, smelly blood. He'd been relieved when Sheriff Phillips sent him outside to search the area around the house for evidence.

And they had found it...an ax...about a half mile from the house...covered with blood and portions of hair.

And that bucket of water on the porch...Looked like someone had washed blood off their hands and then wiped them on a rag that they found lying in the yard. Sort of reminded him of the story of Jesus in the Bible, when Pilate decides he don't want nothin' to do with them Jews crucifying Him. He just sort of washes his hands of the matter...

They'd found three sets of tracks. One set appeared to lead to a Negro's house.

That's why he was still here -- 11 hours later.

Deputy Garland could talk to the Negroes. He had a rapport with the Negroes.

And right now his was one of the few white faces in the crowded room...a cramped, musty little "nightspot" in the woods reeking of stale tobacco, cheap liquor, and sweat. Places like this weren't legal, but sometimes you had to turn a blind eye to things and concentrate on the really important ones -- like these murders, for instance.

At the moment, Calhoun Garland was in deep conversation with several of the revelers. Sometimes he had to strain to hear over the shouts from a nearby craps table.

He could ignore the more ho-hum steady banter...and only once was he really distracted when an attractive and "well-endowed" Negro girl sat herself down at a nearby table. The man sitting next to her suddenly plunged his hand under her skirt. She only smiled, ran her tongue deliberately across her full lips...and shifted.

But all the distractions...all the tiredness aside...his long day was about to pay off.

The Negroes were pointing fingers and talking. Yeah, they sure were talking.

By Tuesday afternoon, nine Negroes were being lodged in the Webster Parish Jail in connection with the attack on Christmas Day of the John Nelson Reeves family in Grove.

Sheriff Phillips knew they weren't all guilty.

But Deputy Garland's investigation the night before had resulted in a lot of finger-pointing and a lot of accusations. And Sheriff Phillips hoped that someone would get nervous and really start spilling his guts.

The suspects had good cause to be nervous.

Four members of a white family were dead -- slaughtered. And a little one, a mere toddler, barely clung to life.

Yeah, they sure as hell ought to be nervous.

Sheriff Phillips would see all the bastards hang to get the killers if he had to. It was 1916 and there'd never been a legal hanging in Webster Parish. But it looked like that might change real soon.

He only prayed that the hangings -- if there were any -- would be legal...that a fair trial could be held. He reckoned he'd do everything in his power to see to that -- it was his duty.

Now if the damned newspapers would just lay off. Damned reporters thought they could solve the case before he could. Just yesterday some high-brow reporter from the Shreveport Journal had declared that "robbery was clearly the motive for the crime."

Hell, they hadn't established that fact yet.

The newspapers were also reporting that Mrs. Reeves had benefited from the opening of a succession -- had gotten $3,500 -- and that it was "kept on the premises."

Now how in the hell do they know that? We don't even know that for sure yet. Damn, damn, damn!!

Maybe I'm just tired, he thought.

He and his men should be tired. They had spent hours combing the area around the Reeves cabin, knocking on doors, and searching houses.

He had talked to each suspect, and then talked to each one again, and then again.

By evening Sheriff Phillips had reached a decision regarding three of the suspects.

"I want you to take Chester Tyson, Mark Peters, and Larkin Stewart over to Caddo Parish...I've already made arrangements with Sheriff Hughes to keep them in his jail."

The two deputies who were the targets of the sheriff's orders looked at each other and nodded. Their wives were used to their long hours, especially lately. It was already dark...and the 60-mile trip to Shreveport and back would take half the night. It was all part of it.

They weren't worried about any trouble. Tyson, Peters, and Stewart didn't seem like dangerous niggers. In fact, of the nine niggers originally brought in, they seemed the least likely of killers.

But facts were facts.

A pistol belonging to old man Reeves had been found under a mattress in Tyson's house, and the ax belonged to him. A bloody pair of overalls had been found at Peters' house, and a bloody shirt at Stewart's. Tracks from the Reeves' home lead directly to Peters.

Looked like they were the ones all right.

But the deputies wondered why Sheriff Phillips was so intent upon moving the three suspects to Caddo Parish. They had a fine two-story jail that was not much more'n 10 years old. The 40 prisoners it housed weren't too crowded. And who gave a God awful damn anyway -- certainly not them -- jail wasn't 'sposed to be a goshed damned fancy hotel, especially for niggers.

'Course the sheriff had been gettin' a lot of calls since the Reeves baby had died that afternoon. His little body was already on its way back to Grove, for burial next to his parents and brothers.

The deputies couldn't help but think about their own kids.

Still, everything in Minden and Webster Parish seemed quiet. The local newspaper, the *Webster Signal*, had even reported the day before that there was no talk of "lynch law" being resorted to should the guilty parties be found.

"It is the general belief that the law will be allowed to take its course," the *Signal* had reported. "The citizens want the murderers punished to the full extent of the law -- but they want it done legally."

The deputies agreed that this was true. In fact, most citizens seemed real upset when the Shreveport newspapers had hinted at the possibility of "mob violence" toward the Negroes. One had even called the *Shreveport Journal* to express disapproval of the big city newspaper's reports of nefarious behavior on the part of Minden and Webster citizens.

Minden was a town whose citizens did not appreciate accusations of probable mob violence coming from "outsiders." Why was it their business anyway?

Things had changed in Minden over the past 20 years, the irate caller had insisted. Lynch laws no longer prevailed.

Both deputies agreed they hadn't seen or heard nothin' -- it probably was just "outside talk."

Guess Sheriff Phillips was just playing it safe.

Caddo Parish Sheriff T.R. Hughes had been more than happy to accommodate Hutch Phillips when he asked to move three murder suspects into his jail.

Sheriffs in Louisiana were loyal to one another, as were most elected officials. You scratch my back, and I'll scratch yours. Call unflattering attention to one elected official -- and you indict them all.

This morning, Sheriff Hughes was mighty anxious to place a call to his colleague in Webster Parish. Seemed a couple of the negra murder suspects had been talking to his deputies. And what they were saying was gonna cause a hell of a stir.

****

Hughes placed his call to Phillips. After their brief conversation, he leaned back, bit the tip from his unlit cigar, spit it aimlessly, tongue-wrestling with a bit that had stubbornly attached itself to his lip...and pondered the significance of what his jailer had told him earlier that morning.

Not only was the surly negra Mark Peters talkin' -- he was pointing a finger at two white men. And the negra Larkin Stewart was backin' his story up.

Only Chester Tyson was still refusin' to talk.

"Bazer!" Sheriff Hughes bellowed.

The deputy had been making a bee-line for the john when the sheriff's barking summons stopped him in his tracks. The call of Mother Nature would just have to wait.

"Call Norton, and then bring me down Peters and Stewart. I desire to have a little talk with those two fellas before Sheriff Phillips arrives."

Norton was Caddo Parish assistant district attorney R.W. Norton. The sheriff felt like he'd be on safer ground with a member of the DA's office present when he questioned the suspects again...and he trusted Norton.

When Hutch Phillips arrived at the Caddo Parish jail later that same day, a deputy was waiting to escort him to a secluded place off Greenwood Road, near Cross Lake on Shreveport's northwest side.

Sheriff Hughes wanted to play it safe.

The Negro suspects were now accusing two white men of murder. He couldn't guarantee that they'd be safe in his jail after word of their accusations got out.

Blaming a white man wouldn't win them any friends.

****

"Boy, why don't you tell Sheriff Phillips here what you told me earlier today," Sheriff Hughes said, peering at Mark Peters from under the brim of his hat. They had gotten out of the car and were making their way towards the lake.

Larkin Stewart, a deputy, and Norton remained behind in the car. Stewart would get his turn later.

Right now, Sheriff Hughes was just interested in seeing if the Negro's stories had changed.

Mark Peters was a big, brutish-looking man. He projected a quiet, contemplative, intelligent strength which had won him many friends among his peers, but intimidated some white folks. Only in his mid-twenties, his haughtiness often led to scrapes with like-minded men. But he usually emerged the victor. Bottom line was...he was idolized by his children, admired by his friends, and feared by his enemies – Negro and White alike.

From the onset, Sheriff Phillips didn't trust him. Hutch Phillips really believed that the eyes were the windows of a man's soul. Mark Peters didn't much mind starin' a man down, but his eyes never gave anything away. They were cold. And that wasn't going to help him in his present circumstances.

According to Peters, a white man, Henry Waller, had mentioned a couple a days before the killings that it would be easy to "get a lot of money."

"Henry tole us that ole man Reeves done got a lot of money to his house...and that it wouldn't be much trouble to get it," Peters said. "He didn't mention murderin' nobody."

Peters talked as the three men walked.

"Then, on that night, Christmas Eve, he and Chester and that white boy Johnie Long, come to my house and called me outside. He tole me we was goin' to ole man Reeves' to play cards...but I knewed he was after that money. So I tole 'im I didn't wanna go...But he just started cussin' and threat'nin. You had to believe the man - he's as mean as they come. Anyway he was carryin' a shotgun, and that white boy was carryin' a pistol, so I

20

figured I didn't have a whole lot of choice. I didn't figure me and Chester with that ax was much against two guns."

Peters paused, sniffed, and wiped his nose on the sleeve of his shirt.

"Yeah, that Henry, he's crazy and I know it..." he said, looking reflective.

After a brief pause, he continued.

"Larkin was stayin' at my house and Henry told me to get him too. He didn't wanna go neither, so Henry threatened him. I just told him to come on. Then Henry, he tole me to go back in the house and fetch him a pair of my shoes 'cause his feet was wet and cold. I brung him my new shoes -- and he put 'em on. They was too big for him...but he wore 'em anyways."

Hoping for a witness to back up Peters' story, Sheriff Phillips pressed the Negro to recall if anyone else might have seen Waller approach his house, or the group of men as they walked to the Reeves cabin.

"No, it was so late, weren't nobody around. We all went on down the road...walkin'..and Henry, he told us to keep quiet, not to talk, lest somebody hear us."

"When we gots to the Reeves place, Henry told me to guard the outside of the house..He told me to lie down on the ground if anybody come around. Then he shoved that shotgun at Chester and took the ax -- he turned it around in his hands lookin' real funny like -- then they went up on to that porch."

"One of 'em shoved open the front door...musta not been locked. I heard a lot of running around and somethin' that sounded like somethin' bein' hit real hard...Me, I took off down that road."

Peters gestured as he talked, using his big hands for emphasis.

"Then I remembered Henry was wearin' my shoes -- and I wanted 'em back. They was new, ya see."

"When I got back to the house, I couldn't hear no more noise. But nobody come out for a spell....least ways that I could see in the front of the house. When they did come out, Henry was awild lookin'...and all bloody..He said, 'We done played hell here tonight. We've murdered all of these people and you sons-of-bitches has got to keep your mouths shut. If'n you don't, I'll kill all of you if it takes me 40 years to do it!' He was crazy, he was.

21

Then, he just washed his hands in a old bucket on that porch like he was washin' up for supper."

"What'd ya'll do then," Sheriff Phillips asked, fishing. "Split up the money?"

"No, sir. Never saw no money. Henry, he just give me back my shoes...and he said for us to go on home...that he'd pay us off later."

Henry Waller, Johnie Long, and Chester Tyson then struck out one way...while Peters and Stewart turned for home.

****

It was winter, but Larkin Stewart was sweating. He sat motionless in the sheriff's car...wondering what was happening to Mark.

As if by rote, he mopped the moisture from his forehead and sighed. Eking out a living from the land in the white man's world was hard on the health...and the soul. Sometimes liquor was the only way to deaden the pain, and Larkin Stewart had had too much of both. That's why he looked much older than his 23 years.

He was wiry and thin, and always seemed to have a cold. On a good day, however, his pasty face would almost shine. Although he possessed a sharp mind, he could neither read nor write. There wasn't much opportunity for schooling among the Negroes in a farming community. So, when the frustration overwhelmed him, he drank.

He had seen Mark walk off with the two white lawmen. For all he knew, he'd never see his friend again. He hadn't heard a gun discharge, so they hadn't shot him...but there was always the lake...or a rope...

He was relieved when the three men returned.

And now it was his turn to take a walk.

****

The setting sun reflected off the rippling surface of Cross Lake, fooling the eye with a look of churning orange molten lava. It's brightness made Larkin Stewart squint.

He told the story like he remembered it.

Only his version placed Mark inside the house.

After the killings, he said, Waller told him and Mark to "go on down the road home...and don't run or act 'spicious. When this thing blows over, I'll pay you off."

"You were in the Minden jail for several days before we brought you over here," Sheriff Phillips commented, pausing. "Why didn't you say anything?"

"Because, Sheriff, we was scared of bein' lynched."

Hutch Phillips eased his lanky frame into a worn chair in the Caddo Sheriff's cramped, warm, and paper-strewn office. It was 3 a.m. The coffee was strong, and not real hot, but hot didn't matter. He just needed it strong.

Earlier in the evening, after hearing Peters and Stewart make their confessions at the lake, they had driven back to Minden to order arrest warrants for the two white men, Henry Waller and Johnie Long.

Then they had personally made the arrests.

Waller had been at home in Germantown asleep when Sheriff Phillips and Deputy Watts came to call with their arrest warrant.

Long was fresh from attending a dance at a neighbor's house, where he'd also planned to spend the night. He was among friends when Sheriff Hughes and Deputy Bazer arrested him.

Neither he nor Waller had resisted.

For obvious reasons, the law officers separated the suspects for the trip back to Shreveport for incarceration.

Waller rode sullenly, not volunteering a word.

Sheriff Hughes, Deputy Bazer, and chauffeur Clyde Toadvin, on the other hand, got the privilege of listening to Johnie Long spill his guts throughout most of the 34-mile trip.

Johnie's lean, tan body was testimony to the fact that he worked outside doing odd jobs on Henry Waller's place, where he lived with his sister, Eva Anderson, her husband, and their children.

Hughes and Bazer had looked at Long's confused, cherub-like face; his high forehead and nervous eyes...and reached the same conclusion -- he was simple-minded. It was only after he began talking that they changed their minds. His uncanny ability to recall details and his articulate, albeit "countrified" speech were not attributes of a simpleton.

Stashed in the back seat, he had initially made no attempts to talk...until the sheriff and his deputy conveniently began to drop hints about Peters' and Stewart's confessions.

Johnie Long had taken his queue...and spilled his guts.

Johnie reckoned it was close to 2 o'clock. It was Christmas, he thought, and here he was, shivering, standing in a thicket within a stone's throw of Mark Peters' house.

His brother's horse was tethered nearby.

So where was Henry? Henry had ordered him to be in Grove by 2 o'clock. He was here, so where was Henry?

Getting here hadn't been easy. If he'd stayed home at Henry's in Germantown, he wouldn't have had a problem getting here. True, the distance from Henry's place in Germantown to old man Reeves' place in Grove was about the same as from his Pa's to Grove. And true, he had planned to attend Mike Martin's wedding up near his Pa's. But if Henry had just let him go on back home after the wedding he would'na had to sneak out of his Pa's house, chase down a horse, and ride 10 miles bareback in the cold and dark...

But Henry had insisted that he stay at his Pa's in Evergreen that night, so he could have an alibi. Whatever that meant. All they was gonna do was play a little cards over to old man Reeves' place. And probably get tanked up -- maybe play some pitch.

Of course Henry had been spoutin' off about taking some money from old man Reeves. Like old man Reeves had any money. He didn't know if he believed those stories about that treasure chest and Miz Maudie inheriting all that money. But if Henry believed it, and Henry wanted to rob old man Reeves, there wasn't much he could do 'bout it.

Henry was his friend. But he was scared of him. He didn't worship Henry like Eva said he did. But he had needed a job...and Henry had given him one. It had been his only chance for independence. Besides, Henry would beat the crap out of him...or might even come near killing him...if he ever crossed him. The devil himself couldn't be as mean as Henry sometimes...

He remembered a couple a years ago when Henry had threatened to kill those children. They'd gone down to the fair in Minden. Henry'd gotten more than a little drunk. On top a that, he was mad -- 'cause he lost money on the horses. Johnie loved fair time, cause the track opened and he loved watching the horses run.

....Anyway, Henry had got mad and chased them children clear down Bayou Avenue...and probably would have killed 'em too if that lady hadn't threatened him with a shotgun.

He mighta been drunk...but he wasn't stupid.

Then there was the time that barn belonging to Henry's Pa had burned down...Well, the barn was supposed to have been full of cotton. But Johnie figured Henry stole the cotton and sold it for profit...then burned the barn to cover his tracks. Fact of the matter was, just a week before the fire, Henry had sold 30 bales of cotton he claimed was picked off his 40 acres. Producing 30 bales off 40 acres was a darn sure agricultural miracle -- everybody knew that. But Henry woulda killed Johnie if he'd made mention of it...

Yep, if Henry wanted to rob old man Reeves, who was he to stand in his way. Old man Reeves was a sorry bootlegging drunk anyway...it's a wonder why Miz Maudie put up with 'em.

It was well after 2 a.m. now.

Where was Henry?

It hadn't been easy...fetching his brother's horse and riding here. Still, it weren't nearly as far as Henry himself was having to ride. He was staying up to Sarepta...like he said...to give himself an alibi.

Johnie and Eva had ridden over to Pa's earlier in the day. Their brother, Jim, lived 'bout a half mile away and they'd visited him that afternoon. Later in the evening, Johnie had attended Mike Martin's wedding over to Ben Kirkley's place. When they'd finally gotten back to Pa's it had been nearly 10 o'clock, and they'd sat around visiting and playing around with the fiddle and harpsichord.

Everybody had gone to bed around 11. It had worried him because he'd had to share a room with his stepbrother, Robert Mobley, and his cousin Lawrence. On top a that, Pa had gone and thrown the latch on the door.

He'd given everybody about an hour to fall asleep. When he finally heard Robert snoring, he crept outa bed, put on his stepbrother's shoes and coat (he'd left his in Pa's room), and tried to sneak out the window. He made so much noise, he just knew the others would wake up. So he scrapped that idea, removed two boards from the floor, and squeezed out.

Catching a horse had been the hard part.

His brother had nailed the stable shut, with his horse inside. He'd been forced to go to the pasture and hem in one of his brother's horses -- and that hadn't been easy.

But he'd finally made it. Now he was here, just like Henry had instructed....

Johnie jumped when he heard a voice -- jolting him from his thoughts. He hadn't heard Henry approach because he was on foot. And he wasn't alone. That nigger, Chester Tyson, was with him.

Henry signaled for Johnie to follow them and they struck off towards Mark's house. The shotgun in Henry's hand and the ax Chester was carrying made him feel a little nervous. But he said nothing.

Mark answered the door.

"Come on, boy, we're going up to old man Reeves' for a drink and a card game," Henry winked at Mark, who was standing in the doorway dressed simply in a pair of ragged thermal bottoms.

Mark declined.

"No, Mr. Henry, we got to get up early and 'sides, I ain't got no money to be spendin' on no cards."

Waller's eyes were gleaming. The corners of his mouth turned faintly upwards into the hint of a smile.

"Now, Mark, you don't need no money. Cause you're gonna be a rich man when you leave old man Reeves'. I promised Chester here the same thing. He's getting married tomorrow, and he's gonna need a little stash. I told him I felt real lucky tonight...And that he just might benefit from my lucky streak."

He had paused on the word l-u-c-k-y.

Waller gestured towards a dark figure who had suddenly appeared behind Peters. His hand still gripped the shotgun.

"So, boy, you get your friend there, and you get me a pair of your shoes, and you come on. I don't think you want to turn me down a second time."

Mark understood. So did Larkin Stewart.

After a few moments, Mark and Larkin emerged from the house. Mark handed Henry a pair of shoes, which he promptly swapped with his own. They looked new.

The five men headed off towards the Reeves' place.

What struck Johnie as peculiar when they arrived was the fact that there were no lights on in the Reeves' house -- except one in the very back. Everything sure was quiet considering they'd been invited to play cards and booze it up.

Henry's up to no good, Johnie remembered thinking.

His fears were confirmed when Henry took the ax from Chester and instructed the Negro to stay put outside. He sent

Larkin around back to "watch the road." Johnie and Mark were to follow him.

The three of them walked up to the porch. Henry half-heartedly called out to Reeves. When there was no response, Henry tried the door. It was unlocked.

The three men entered the house -- Waller first, followed by Peters, and then Long.

Johnie remembered vividly Waller creeping up to the bed where old man Reeves lay sleeping, snoring loudly.

Without warning, Waller raised the ax. It came down with a force so hard that the top of Reeves' head exploded, splashing brains, blood and flesh against the pillow and nearby wall. Again Waller struck. And again.

"God-damn!" Peters stammered, running from the room.

Johnie stood frozen in his tracks. He wanted to run...to follow Mark...but he couldn't move. Waller then turned...his eyes were glazed...cold.

There were several children sleeping peacefully on a pallet in front of the fireplace in the same room. Waller raised the ax. It came down. Johnie still could not move.

Waller was possessed.

Johnie heard a child cry out. Then another.

Suddenly, Mrs. Reeves was running past him and out the door. Henry was right behind her....looking like a madman...

He didn't see what happened next.

Johnie was numb. He had yet to will his feet to move. Chester entered the house and walked to a small utility room. He came out carrying an old chest. By the time Johnie managed to walk the distance of the room, and out onto the porch, Chester was forcing open the cranky old chest. Johnie saw him remove a pistol from it...but nothing else.

Then Henry was standing on the porch surveying them. He had washed his blood-soaked hands in a bucket of water and was now drying them on an old rag.

He tossed it into the yard.

"By God, we've played hell here tonight, gentlemen," he said. "If any one of you breathes one word of this to anyone...I'll kill you. You know I will...if it takes me 40 years to do it."

****

Johnie stopped talking.

28

Tharump....tharump...tharump....

The Model T's hard rubber tires labored clumsily over a road God had meant only for horses and wagons.

Sheriff Hughes cleared his throat, ending the nervous silence that had overcome the occupants.

"Sheriff," Johnie suddenly spoke again, looking out from frightened eyes, "Are you taking me to the same place you're takin' Henry? 'Cause if you are -- he'll kill me for sure. You "You'll be safe," Hughes said reassuringly, wondering why the kid was so afraid to confront the accused. "You won't be in the same part of the jail, and my deputies won't let anyone near you."

It wouldn't be the only time Johnie asked about confronting Waller during the long trip from Germantown to Shreveport.

Later that night, sitting in Sheriff Hughes' office, surrounded by officers of the law, Johnie retold his story.

While the man he feared more than anyone else in the world, Henry Waller, sat brooding in a jail cell just a few doors down, Johnie Long repeated his confession.

It was recorded...and signed.

****

Sheriff Phillips and Deputy Watts lingered in Shreveport just long enough to see their two prisoners booked into the Caddo Parish Jail. Then they drove east toward Minden, straight into the face of a meekly rising sun, and they discussed whether or not there was reason to continue holding the remaining Negroes. Sheriff Phillips said he was seriously considering setting them free.

So far, no money had been found to establish robbery as a motive for the killings -- despite what the newspapers said.

Chester Tyson and Henry Waller were still vehemently denying any connection whatsoever with the murders.

In fact, Waller claimed that he was 20 miles away visiting relatives in Sarepta on the night of the killings.

Phillips would have his deputies check out his story later today -- after they got some rest. Several Caddo deputies had also been assigned the same task.

A "frame-up" was not totally out of the question. But he certainly had his doubts. He didn't know how the Negroes and that boy, Long, could have concocted such an elaborate scheme. Quite

29

frankly he didn't think they had the stuff it would have taken...And, more importantly, he knew a little about Waller's past.

Any way you looked at it, the investigation was far from over.

And people were going to get more and more stirred up, of that he was sure.

Back in his office, Sheriff Phillips pulled off his boots and stretched his legs out tentatively. He was being cautious because the bare hint of a cramp had begun nagging at his calf - the price he was paying for riding in an automobile most of the night.

He was still massaging the leg and deep in thought when the dayshift jailer sidled into the office. The deputy scratched his crotch and looked for a place to snub his cigarette before it burned his yellowed fingers. Finding none, he flipped it onto the floor and flattened it with the toe of his boot.

"Sheriff, one of the niggers wants a chat with you," he said finally. "Want me to fetch him for you?"

Phillips nodded absent-mindedly, pondering the length of time it would take a man on horseback to ride from Sarepta to Grove...

Anderson Heard, one of the Negroes still being held for questioning in the Reeves case, was ushered into the room.

Next to the deputy, he appeared small and timid. He barely stood 5'5" tall and didn't wear his 140 pounds well. He could have been 25 or he could have been 50. Tiny, mouselike ears hugged his head closely -- a head that kept bobbing up and down as he waited for the sheriff to notice him.

Which he finally did.

The mole on his lower lip quivered as he confessed to being at the Reeves place Christmas morning.

Sheriff Phillips shook his head and stared at the Negro...then exchanged a long look with Deputy Watts, who had come into the room seconds before the confession and was warming his hands around a hot cup of coffee. The look they exchanged was one of skepticism.

Why had none of the other suspects mentioned Heard in their confessions? Not one of them had mentioned a sixth party.

The sheriff sighed and said nothing. Ignoring the Negro, he stared out the window across Back Street to Main and the spindly elm and ash trees decorating the nearby courthouse lawn -- trees

30

groomed perfectly for hangings. That possibility was looming ever more closely.

Unconsciously he ran his hand over tired eyes and rubbed his temples. Why, at this point, would someone else confess? This guy had to be really stupid to worry about getting fingered by the others at this late date. Why confess now?

The whole thing bothered him...something was just not right. He had three people confessing, and two more strenuously denying any part. And, as closely as their stories matched...could any one of them be lying?

The case was getting a lot of press. Articles had appeared daily in both Shreveport papers and weekly in the local newspaper. Could an imaginative person read those accounts and fill in any blanks? And why on earth would anyone want to admit to such acts of butchery? Were any of his suspects that imaginative...that intelligent...that stupid?

Hell, most of 'em couldn't even read!

Were they smart enough to frame Waller?

Because Waller seemed to have a pretty damned good alibi.

Sheriff Phillips finally spoke, his gaze falling on his trusted deputy.

"Let's call Drew," was all he said.

Later, seated in the District Attorney's Office, Heard related his account of the Christmas morning killing spree.

Only his version placed the ax in Chester Tyson's hand.

According to Heard, the two "white men" had nothing whatsoever to do with the murders.

****

Heard was returned to his cell.

Phillips, Drew and Watts discussed the possibility that the Negro might be slightly mentally retarded. He had not been that coherent...and had made only a few points, introducing nothing new to the case.

"When Detective Price from Shreveport gets here later this afternoon, I want you to take our boy, Mr. Heard, out to the Reeves' place and walk him through everything," Phillips instructed Watts. "Find out what he knows and doesn't know."

He leaned closer to Watts, but remained in earshot of Drew.

"I'm not sure this negra has all his marbles. So don't help him any. And don't let Price coach him either. Just find out what he knows."

****

Detective Teddy Price from Caddo Parish made it obvious from the "get-go" that he felt himself superior to the "country bumpkins" who were already working on the case.

The "Napoleonesque," red-haired, quasi-Sherlock Holmes was a bundle of nervous energy. He thought he was important -- even if the world didn't agree.

"Sheriff Hughes might have great respect for these bumpkins," Price thought to himself enroute to the murder scene with Deputy Watts. "But I, Detective Ted Price of the Price Brothers Detective Agency, will just have to show them how an investigation is supposed to be handled."

Arriving in Grove, they walked Heard around the murder scene, watching him closely. The suspect immediately pointed out the area where he thought the ax had landed after it was allegedly tossed by the killer.

"Close...but no cigar," Watts reflected. "The negra could have overheard others talking in jail and guessed about where the murder weapon had been found."

Price was another story.

"Looks like we got ourselves another boy," the cocky little detective boasted, as if he'd had something to do with Heard's unfortunate and untimely confession.

His hat rose and fell agitatedly on his head as he talked.

"We'll take him to Shreveport...I've got a few 'plants' already in place...talking to the other prisoners...I'm gonna solve this case...yes, sir...you can bet old Ted Price is gonna solve this case."

Price, as pompous as he was, did have good instincts. Those extrasensory feelings were telling him there was more to this case than met the eye.

Watts only shook his head at the bantam rooster with the private investigator's license and directed his prisoner to the waiting car.

"We've already 'cracked' this case without your help, thank you -- you son-of-a-bitch," he thought to himself. "All you're gonna do is muddy the waters with your 'plants.' Sheriff Phillips already has enough evidence to turn over to the Grand Jury -- and they can decide who goes to trial."

That day couldn't come soon enough.

But the Grand Jury wasn't scheduled to convene until January 9, unless they were called into special session. The judge could do that.

But it wasn't very likely.

Sunday, December 31, 1916
Webster Parish Courthouse
Minden, Louisiana

Sheriff Phillips tossed the Sunday newspaper on his desk and walked to the window. Below him lay Minden's central business district, which was situated on top of a hill, gently sloping off into railroad yards on the west, a large cotton ginning concern to the south, Broadway and old ante-bellum homes to the northeast, and dense, piney woods wherever else the eye might choose to rest.

Main Street was quiet...and somewhat depressing. Spindly naked fingers of young trees cast their crooked shadows onto the muddy earthen thoroughfare that had served as the area's central mercantile route since 1836.

Most everyone was in church.

Standing at just the right angle, he could barely make out the steeple of the First Methodist Church. If he hadn't had so much on his mind, he'd be in church himself, sitting with his family, willing to take up the offering, or whatever else needed to be done.

But preaching wasn't on his mind this morning. He didn't think his brain could take more challenges right now. The Reeves case had more twists and turns than Lake Bistineau had sloughs...and that was a lot.

If Henry Waller had, in fact, spent the night in Sarepta, he had a pretty stout alibi. And Sheriff Hughes tended to believe Waller's story...was even leaning towards a frame-up against him by the negras.

Phillips had read a letter the Caddo sheriff had written to Waller, who had been moved to a jail 120 miles south in Alexandria for protection. Sheriff Hughes said a man had a right to know developments in his own case, whether favorable or unfavorable. And the latest developments were certainly favorable. Phillips as much as agreed.

That wasn't all. Several reputable citizens of Sarepta had come forward to swear that Waller was with them the night of the murders, not in Grove.

Phillips glanced toward the newspaper on his desk.

One of them, Justice of the Peace J.H.C. Coyle, had even called the *Shreveport Journal* long distance to declare that statements connecting Waller with the Reeves' murders were untrue.

Mr. Coyle had declared that Waller was in Sarepta -- 20 miles from the scene of the tragedy -- during the whole of last Sunday night (Christmas Eve), and that fact could be established by a half dozen or more reliable witnesses.

"If we believed Mr. Waller guilty," the *Journal* had quoted Coyle as saying, "we would be the first to demand that he be punished. But we know he cannot possibly be guilty, for he was unquestionably in Sarepta throughout the night of the tragedy."

Sheriff Phillips sighed, still staring out the window. The fire glowing in the belly of the blacksmith shop on Pine Street looked warm and inviting, almost comforting. It was one of the last blacksmith shops of its kind still operating in town. Will Fuller had just announced plans to build a new stone garage at Main and Broadway to repair automobiles. Would Chaffe's blacksmith shop follow suit?

The thought made Sheriff Phillips sad. Things were changing too fast, that was for sure.

And along with progress, he mused, came more crime - with bigger and better ways to commit it.

You can't even be safe in your own bed on Christmas eve, he thought, and sighed again.

From somewhere below the hill, the melancholy mixture of a train's whistle and its powerful, humming, thrusting engines fractured the Sabbath day stillness.

His lips formed the words.

"Happy New Year."

Will Lloyd was a detective...a good detective.

He had only one problem.

He was a Negro. And, as such, his business wasn't exactly thriving.

So when Earl Price of the Price Detective Agency called and said he had a job for him, Lloyd jumped at the chance.

His mission was to become a "plant" inside the Texarkana, Arkansas jail.

He would share a cell with Chester Tyson, who had been moved once again as a precautionary measure by Sheriff Phillips.

The idea of being in jail...of sharing a dingy, confined space with anyone, much less a suspected murderer, didn't appeal to Lloyd. But, work was work...and it sure wouldn't hurt his private eye business if he got Tyson to confess.

He knew Price had already applied the same tactics to Mark Peters and Larkin Stewart, who had been transferred from the Caddo Parish Jail to the lock-up in Mansfield, Louisiana on New Years Day. They had openly talked with the "plant" inside the jail. But to Price's disappointment, they once again implicated a white man, Henry Waller.

Price had considered using the same technique with Anderson Heard, but everything pointed to his being a few bricks short of a load. They hadn't even bothered to move him from the jail in Minden.

So the Shreveport detective was pinning all his hopes of solving this case without a trial on Chester Tyson. If Tyson confessed without implicating anyone else, and if he then convinced his co-conspirators to plead guilty...Price would be a hero. His status among his peers would be greatly elevated...and he'd find favor where he could use it best in his profession - law enforcement, the judges, the district attorney...the possibilities were endless.

Price was really counting on Will Lloyd to crack Tyson, who was still the only member of the quartet who had not confessed.

Tyson was his ace in the hole -- his ticket to success.

"Lawd, Lawd...what they gonna do ta me...what they gonna do ta me?"

Will Lloyd brought his knees up to his chest, hugging himself and rocking back and forth on the hard cell bunk.

He continued wailing for another four or five minutes before his cellmate, Chester Tyson, asked if he was all right.

"They gonna beat me...prob'ly poke me likes a pig...I know they is...They gonna do awful thangs ta me...they probably gonna hang me right here in this cell...the man say he gonna cut off my dick and feed it to his dog...I'll prob'ly be wishing I was dead when they finish with me....Lawd, Lawd..."

"What you done to deserve all that?" Chester asked. "I been in one jail after 'nuther durin' the last week, and they ain't threatened me like that."

"I done real damn bad...I don' know what you did, but it cain't be bad as what I done...No...cain't be nearly dat bad."

"What'd you do?" Chester asked.

"Done gone and killed two deputies...Was trying to rob a bank and they just got in the way...it was them or me...so I shot 'em...And you know if you cross a policeman, you gone pay...Lawd I'm scairt...what they gone do ta me?"

Lloyd was warming to his role...and he knew he was convincing.

"See what I mean...you ain't done nothin' so bad. What you done? Why you here?"

Chester stared off into nowhere for a few seconds and Lloyd thought he had lost him...Damn! He wasn't looking forward to spending the night in this jail cell trying vainly to get Tyson to confess.

"You right, man, I didn' do nothin' as bad as killin' no lawman."

Lloyd's heart stopped. Was Tyson going to confess? He buried his head in his arms and continued his side-to-side rocking motion.

By this time, Chester was pacing the small cell, rubbing his hands together for warmth. He had thrown a shabby wool blanket over his shoulders to ward off the cold, but the draft from a tiny nearby window was damp and chilling. Beyond it, he could see nothing by drab gray sky.

"You heard 'bout that Reeves family got themselves killed up north of Minden?" Tyson finally spoke, his teeth chattering as much from nerves as the cold.

Lloyd could feel his cellmate's eyes peering at him...but he still didn't look up. He hesitated to answer...not sure if Tyson would be more apt to tell him about the murder if he knew about it...or if he feigned ignorance.

He decided.

"I done heard a little somethin' about it...I was playin' craps down in Shiney and heard somethin' about it. But what you got ta do with that?"

"I didn' kill those white people, no suh. But I guarded that house while them white men hacked up that family. And you know, they gonna hang me for it. Shoulda run when I knowed what was goin' on...but I was too scared. That white man Waller...he's a mean son of a bitch...I mean, he'd a killed me fa sure. Anyways, I was gettin' married Christmas Day...and Waller, he promised he'd give me some money...I needed that money…and I figured old man Reeves owed me more than he ever paid me."

"Now I'm just gonna hang for somethin' a damned sorry white bastard did. Took me off to this place the day after my wedding - broke my little girl's heart."

For a moment, neither man spoke.

"Well..," Lloyd was now looking at Tyson with renewed interest. Fact was, he believed him. "Well...what you got to lose by tellin' them lawmen that you was just standin' guard? You needs to tell 'em you was scared...and that the white man did that killin'...hell, what you got to lose...your already 'fraid you gonna hang -- if they don't cut off your balls first!"

Chester closed his eyes tight and opened them again, wide. He rubbed his hands over his face. He wished he could rub away everything that had happened over the past week. Everything, that is, except his union with Josephine. She was the one good thing that had happened to him. How could he have let this happen?

He finally spoke.

"You know it won't make one bit a difference if I say I did it or didn't do it. We're colored. And you know what that means in a court of law. White people are gonna believe white people...they ain't gonna believe no colored man."

Will Lloyd did know. But he had to keep trying.

"That's just it," he continued, sitting upright on the side of his bunk and facing his cellmate. "That's just it -- it probably won't make no bit of difference."

Then, catching himself becoming too excited, he paused. It was obvious that Tyson was no dummy. And if his cellmate perceived him as becoming too interested in his situation, he'd become suspicious. He needed to tone down his approach...maybe talk a little more about his own troubles. Then he could divert the conversation back to the confession.

"I knows some white folks who treat me fair," he finally said. "You know, not all white folks hate negras. 'Course it ain't gonna do me no good. Like I said, I killed the man. I'm a sure fire son-of-a-bitch gonner."

He stood and walked to the cell bars. He leaned his head against the cold steel and sighed heavily.

"I guess I deserve what they gonna dish out to me. But you? What you got to lose by tellin' the truth? They can only kill you once."

Chester looked thoughtful.

"Maybe you're right," he said finally, nodding at Lloyd. "I guess, in the back of my mind, I knew we was up to no good. But I figured, as much money as old man Reeves took off me in poker...guess I figured he owed me. But it wasn't right - and I knew it."

Lloyd let him continue.

"At least you right about not having anything to lose. They probably gonna hang me anyway."

Lloyd shook his head, feeling uncomfortably sorry for Chester Tyson.

"Next time the man come by, why don't you tell him you want to talk to the sheriff? Cain't do you no harm."

When the jailer appeared, bringing their evening meal, Tyson did as Will Lloyd advised.

He repeated his confession to the sheriff, the jailer and another witness.

His confession put the ax in Henry Waller's hand.

And Teddy Price was terribly disappointed.

Friday, January 19, 1917
Grove Christian Church
Webster Parish, Louisiana

Luke Grigsby wasn't an ordained preacher, but most folks considered him the next best thing. He sure wasn't afraid to stand up in front of a group of his peers and speak his mind. On top of that, he was good at organizing things.

That's why he was here now, standing in the pulpit of the Grove Christian Church.

The small sanctuary was home to Baptists and Methodists on alternating Sundays. Folks belonging to those "off-brand" religions - the Episcopalians, Presbyterians, Catholics, and "others" had to travel the four or five miles into Minden to worship. Or, like the Church of Christ followers, meet in someone's home.

On this particular occasion, the tiny house of worship was full to overflowing and the subject was far more controversial than what color to paint the fence around the cemetery.

The cold-blooded, brutal murders that had taken place virtually in their own backyards had been the single topic of discussion in the small community for the past three weeks.

How could it happen?

Could it ever happen again?

Most importantly, what could be done to make sure it never happened again?

For the God-fearing people of Grove, the murder of the Reeves family represented more than a challenge for law enforcement. The Reeves children had played side-by-side with their own precious sons and daughters. They had gone to sleep on Christmas eve night feeling secure and protected.

Could their own children feel so safe now? Would they trust them, as adults, to protect them? And could they?

Some action needed to be taken...some assurances given, not only to their own children, but to the outside world that was so busy looking in. The newspapers were full of the murderous tale...it seemed as though the reporters couldn't get enough.

The latest reports revealed that, on the previous Saturday, the Webster Parish Grand Jury had handed down indictments against four Negro suspects, charging them with the murder of John Nelson Reeves.

40

The two white men implicated by the Negroes remained incarcerated, Waller in Shreveport and Long in Alexandria.

The fact that the alleged killers lived and worked right here in their own community shocked and appalled the citizens of Grove. Henceforth...the call for action...

"We need a little order in here now folks," Grigsby said, his voice barely rising above the din of neighborly chat. Someone handed him a pocketknife, which he rapped repeatedly against the hollow, wooden lectern. The room gradually grew quiet as people began directing their attention toward the speaker.

"All right, we've got a lot of things to discuss, but first, I think we should decide how we're going to organize as a community. Has anyone got any suggestions?"

"We want to hear what you've got to say, Luke," someone called from the back.

"Yeah, what do you suggest we do?"

There followed a boisterous exhibition of support for Grigsby, who agreed to become chairman of the group, whatever form it took. After brief discussion, M. D. Wren was appointed to serve as secretary. He would keep notes and carry any and all correspondence to the newspapers and court officials.

"I believe that we must form some resolutions," Grigsby offered, after the parliamentary activities were completed. "We must, first and foremost, inform the world that we do not condone the commission of crimes of any kind within our neighborhood. The way I see it, that's why we're here. Because, by not meeting like this, we're sending a message to the world that we don't care. And I, for one, am not willing to do that - because I do care!"

The crowd echoed total agreement.

For the next hour, Grigsby milked the crowd...the ideas flowed...Wren's pen hand seldom slowed.

"I think we absolutely must express our sorrow for what happened, and our sympathy," Miss Annie Wiley boldly offered, standing. "These people were our neighbors...we can't let ourselves get so bent on protectin' our reputation that we forget to mourn the dead."

"Miss Annie's right," another agreed. "We got to let 'em know we sympathize. And another thing...we got to let 'em know we want justice - no matter who the killers turn out to be...I don't care if a fella's got a big family name or's poor as dirt, and quite

41

frankly, I don't care whether he's negra or white...as Christians, we got to see justice done."

"That's a good point," Grigsby agreed. "And to go a step further, we should let the authorities know that we are willing to cooperate with them. Some of you may get called as witnesses. Our sheriff and the court must know that they can count on us - that we are willing to testify. Because, remember, the suspects they've got right now are also our neighbors. Some of us may be called as character witnesses...who knows."

"What if the same thing happens here 'at happened over in Mississippi coupla weeks ago?" J. V. Braselton asked. "You know, them boys forced their way into that jail and grabbed that negra...took him out and hanged him, remember? And he had'n even been tried yet...they just decided he was guilty of rapin' that girl 'cause the sheriff arrested him."

Everyone seemed to have an opinion on the matter, and everybody began talking at once. Grigsby gave the lectern a few sharp raps with the butt of the knife.

"People, people. We know as Christians that we can't - we won't - let that happen here. I sure don't think Sheriff Phillips will tolerate anything from a mob. And, to return to the point about color...or family influence, I have faith that the courts will mete out justice as needs be. And, perhaps, in one of our resolutions, we should express our confidence in the sheriff and the court..."

Everyone agreed.

Wren wrote furiously.

Annie Wiley returned to her feet.

"So after all is said and done, what will we have accomplished, Luke? You know, and everybody in this room knows, that we've got bad elements in our community. Any time of the day or night, you can find boozin' and gamblin' and worse, right here!" she gestured wildly. "There's a move on in this great nation to outlaw demon liquor -- we ought to take a stand right here and now to support that movement! People seem to think the law wasn't meant for them, what with the bootleggin' and gamblin' and (pardon me, Lord!) prostitution going on...This is our opportunity, Luke, to show the world that there are God-fearing, law-abiding people here in Grove, Louisiana! This is our chance to put a stop to it all!"

People clapped and whooped...Miss Annie's pentecostal spirit had been unleashed upon the crowd.

Wren gave up trying to write. He looked questioningly at Grigsby, his pen suspended motionless above the tablet of notes. Then he shrugged. Grigsby nodded solemnly, but said nothing, letting the crowd work out its own frustrations. After a few moments, the din began to fade and all eyes focused, once again, on the chairman.

"Thank you, Miss Annie," Grigsby said, walking from behind the lectern. "You've brought us to another very important resolution. This community does have problems, as do all communities. What I suggest is that we pledge - in this resolution that we are sending to the newspapers - that we pledge to work toward moral and civic reform for ALL communities; that we will work, not just today or for the duration of what trials are to come, for the suppression of crime and immoral conduct in our community and every community; and for the punishment of anyone...anyone...who acts in a way unbecoming a Christian community."

"So resolved!" Miss Annie hollered.

"That's exactly what we need to say," another offered.

"Yeah, we knew we picked the right man for the job."

The defense table where Chester Tyson, Mark Peters, Anderson Heard, and Larkin Stewart sat huddled with court-appointed attorney D. Webster Stewart was uncharacteristically uncluttered.

Under normal circumstances, the desktop would have been littered with piles of paperwork, stacks of reference books, and bits and pieces of paper bearing notes hastily scribbled and passed between defendant and counselor.

But the desk was clean...despite the string of witnesses who had already testified.

Spectators hung on every word uttered by Jewel Johnson, who had discovered the bodies; and Sheriff Phillips, who investigated the crime.

There followed after them a host of witnesses whose testimony was relative, but not quite as interesting.

Will Life, bookkeeper for Webb Hardware Company, identified the Reeves pistol as one that had been purchased in May of 1912 from a St. Louis hardware firm and sold to Henry Hanson.

Hanson confirmed the purchase and said he later traded it to Hamp Mitchell, a Negro, for another gun.

Hamp Mitchell traded the gun to his brother, John, for a pair of shoes.

And John Mitchell swapped the weapon to John Nelson Reeves for a shotgun, some gears, and $7.50 in cash.

Deputy Bob Carstarphen identified the pistol as the one he found between mattresses in Chester Tyson's home on Christmas Day.

Will Bronson, who was present, testified that Earl Taylor took the gun and turned it over to Sheriff Phillips.

Sheriff Phillips confirmed on the stand that, indeed, this was the pistol Earl Taylor had given him.

Identification of the ax followed basically the same procedure.

Will Lane identified the ax as the one found the day after the murder near a stump in a strip of woods three-quarters of a mile from the Reeves place. It was bloody and smeared with human hair.

Marks on a sapling and stump indicated to Lane that the ax had been tossed there from a distance. He said he and Bill Jones found the ax when they were following tracks leading from the Reeves house.

Zach Martin identified the ax as having belonged to John Tyson, late father of Chester Tyson.

Will Hawkins, who chopped wood for Tyson's mother, Mariah Tyson, identified the ax as one that was on her place December 23, but was missing Christmas Day.

Mrs. Tyson was ill and could not attend the trial of her son to testify to the ownership of the alleged murder weapon.

Confessions formed the bulk of the case for the prosecution.

"Sheriff Hughes, your deputies were present for the confessions of Mark Peters and Larkin Stewart, were they not? And you also witnessed these confessions?"

Drew directed his question to the Caddo Parish sheriff.

"Yes. Three of the negras admitted, at different times, to being at the killings."

"Obviously they could have not said anything. Why do you think they confessed?"

"I certainly can't say, Mr. Drew. But this Court can rest assured that neither me, nor any of my men, threatened, mistreated, or promised them anything for their confessions...only protection from a lynch mob."

"Were these confessions witnessed by anyone outside law enforcement?"

"Yes, sir. Caddo Assistant District Attorney R. W. Norton sat in on a couple...and I believe you were present at one yourself, sir."

"These defendants," Drew pointed to the Defense table, "incriminated themselves, didn't they?"

"Objection," Stewart drawled. "I don't see how the sheriff can speak for every man at this table."

Judge Sandlin agreed, sustaining the motion.

But Drew had won the round. He ceded the questioning to Stewart, satisfied.

"Sir, when you questioned my clients, did you instruct them regarding incrimination?"

"Absolutely," Sheriff Hughes answered. "We instructed the prisoners not to incriminate any innocent person."

"And did any one of them implicate Anderson Heard."

"No....I can't recall that they did."

The defense attorney's face brightened.

He had been content to focus his defense effort on having Anderson Heard declared mentally incompetent -- too "dim-witted" to be taken seriously. Testimony that he wasn't even there was better.

In truth, Heard's wide-eyed and fearless disregard of the current situation should have gone a long way towards convincing the judge, jury, and courtroom of his simple-mindedness -- or his innocence.

Two of Heard's former employers, B. F. Carr and Lawrence Newsom, had already testified that, as an employee, the Negro had to be told exactly what to do, regardless of how many times he'd already performed a particular job.

"Would you say that Anderson Heard is a half-witted Negro?" Stewart had asked Carr.

"Well, sir, I'd say he was dull. But he knows how to work and obey. I don't know that I'd say he was half-witted.....maybe easily led would be more like it."

Newsom, on the stand, had described Heard as "simple."

Those weren't exactly the answers the defense attorney wanted.

But he settled for them...and they worked.

When District Attorney Drew later objected to Stewart's motion to have his client's initial confession disqualified on the grounds of mental incompetence, Judge Sandlin swiftly overruled. This ruling, Stewart told reporters later, had given him hope that, while he might not save the man from a murder conviction, it might at least spare him the noose.

But Drew still wasn't buying.

****

Shad Zillener, an elderly Negro man, sat in the witness chair looking frail and scared. Drew's tone was soothing.

"Mr. Shad, tell us about Christmas day, when you were overtaken on the road by Anderson Heard."

46

"Well, Mr. Drew...I'd just come from the Reeves place...and I told Anderson what a terrible sight I done seen. Anderson looked kinda funny and said he'd done been over there but hadn't done nothin' -- said they'd offered him 50 cents for going..but he didn't go til they offered him $10."

"Thank you, Mr. Shad."

"I just have a few questions for this witness," Webster Stewart didn't rise from his seat. "When did Anderson say he'd been over at the Reeves home...did he say he'd been at the Reeves home on Sunday night precisely?"

"No, suh, he didn't exactly say...I just thought he meant he'd been over to the Reeves the night of the murders...Sunday night."

"But he didn't say precisely Sunday night...?"

"No, suh."

On cross examination, Adversus Heard testified that his brother had left home Sunday evening for Chester Tyson's...saying that he was going to attend Chester's wedding the next day.

"When he come back home Monday, he told me that Chester offered to sell him a pistol and a watch...and had offered him $10 to go over there."

"And did he take him up on his offer?" Stewart asked.

"No, he said he didn't go...said Chester had told him he was going to old man Reeves to play some cards...and he didn't want to go."

"Mr. Heard, do you think your brother is a smart man?"

Drew objected.

"Your Honor, one can hardly expect a man to speak objectively about his own brother's intelligence."

"Your Honor, suh, I don't mind answering the question...suh, I don't think my brother Anderson's at all smart...No suh. Facts is he's kinda empty-headed...that's if'n you ask me, suh..."

****

Larkin Stewart was the first of the accused to take the stand on his own behalf.

He appeared less frightened than his co-defendants and anxious to testify.

Time spent behind bars had made his normally lean face appear more gaunt than ever. He looked nervously around the room.

"Now, Larkin," the burly Defense attorney drawled, standing before the witness, "where were you the night the Reeves murders took place?"

It was a stock question...one intended to relax the defendant. Four witnesses had already placed Larkin at his brother-in-law's house the night of the killings. Yet when pressed to swear positively that he did not leave the house once everyone retired at nine, not even the defendant's wife, Pearl, or sister, Dessie, could say with certainty. Pearl did, however, assure the court that she would have known if her husband had left the house for any reason.

"Well, suh, I rodes a horse for Mr. Jack Monzingo Sunday mornin', and thens me and my wife went on over to Ernest and Dessie's place Sunday evenin'. We's stayed the night there."

"That's your sister and your brother-in-law?"

"Yes, suh."

"And you never left the house? You didn't get out of bed after everyone else retired and leave your brother-in-law's house for any reason?"

"No, suh," Larkin replied, shaking his head from side to side. "No, suh, I show did'n."

"In addition to you and your wife, and your sister and her husband, there was a boarder at the McGee's who saw you too, was there not?"

"Yes, suh. That'd be Sam Veal, he's roomin' with mah sister and Ernest...he knowed that I stayed there, too."

"Larkin...were you present when the Reeves family was murdered?"

"No, suh...I never killed nobody."

"No more questions, your honor."

Then it was Drew's turn to question the witness.

"Why did you tell those deputies in the Shreveport jail...and Sheriff Hughes....and Sheriff Phillips...that you were present at the murders?" Drew's approach was direct...he lost no time getting down to business.

"That wuz Mark.....," Larkin Stewart's head bobbed up and down and he fidgeted nervously with the brim of his hat, which

48

was resting in his lap. He avoided looking at Mark Peters. "He done told a story in the jail house. He done said that he 'n Johnie Long, and Mr. Waller they done killed them people...said I was there...an' I don know why I went along with dat story...jus did....but I was'n there...an' I didn't kill nobody. An' I cain't face my God with a lie on my lips...cain't cause nobody to suffer."

"But Dave Frazier testified earlier that he had found two work shirts in the bottom of a clothes barrel at your house several days after the killings, didn't he? And those shirts had blood on them, didn't they? But Mr. Frazier couldn't swear for certain that those were your shirts, Mr. Stewart. Were those your shirts?" Drew asked.

Larkin Stewart looked confused.

"Yes, suh...they was my shirts alright."

"And they did have blood on them, didn't they?"

"Yes, suh. They had blood on 'em from a nose bleed...I had me a nosebleed and I wiped my nose with them shirts. That happened Saturday...and I changed them shirts Saturday."

"A nose bleed?" Drew feigned concern. "Do you get nose bleeds often, Mr. Stewart?"

"No, suh, onliest sometimes."

Drew leaned close to the defendant.

"Did Henry Waller or anyone ever say anything to you about killing Mr. Reeves?"

"No, suh," Larkin Stewart shook his head. "No, suh. Nobody said nothin' 'bout killin' nobody. And that's the truth...An' I shore wants to die with the truth on my lips."

****

Days of incarceration had not diminished Mark Peters' rogue appearance. He unconsciously gnawed on his finger, seldom looking up, refusing to show that he was intimidated by the presence of armed deputies.

He had found few friends in the courtroom. Not that he needed any. He admitted being present when the murders took place.

His wife had predictably testified that he was at home all Sunday night, and that she would have known had he left the house. Several others said they had seen Peters Sunday, but only until late afternoon.

Mark's friend, Felix Terrell, did more damage than good.

49

"Mark and his suster, dey come over to my place on Christmas mornin'," Terrell recalled. "Mark, he acted real nervous. He pulled offen his shoes...whittled on a winder...then he went on outside and stayed coupla minutes. When he come back in, dat's when he tole us he'd heard the Reeves been a murdered over da night. Mark, he acted kinda nervous...he weren't actin' like he was 'spose ta.'"

Terrell's wife, Emma Lou, corroborated her husband's story, adding that Mark had looked anxious and distant.

Dug Lunsford, a white farmer and neighbor of the Reeves, testified that he, G. W. Morgan, and Ernest Morgan had followed tracks from the Reeves' place to Mark Peters' house. The Morgans were also neighbors.

"We asked Mark Peters' boy if the tracks leading from the Reeves house to his belonged to his daddy, and he said they did," Lunsford told the court.

"And what did you find when you entered the house?" Drew asked.

"A pair of tan shoes...they had blood stains all over 'em," Lunsford answered.

"Objection, your honor," Stewart said, not bothering to rise, "Witness is not an expert...he has no way of knowing that the stains on those shoes were blood."

"Sustained, reword your question or proceed to something else," Judge Sandlin directed.

"Were these the same shoes that Dr. Butler examined earlier today?" Drew asked Lunsford.

"Yes, sir."

Dr. Willis P. Butler was the Caddo Parish coroner and a respected chemist and bacteriologist. He had conducted testing on blood samples provided to him by Drew and the Webster sheriff. He had received the samples on December 30, and it had taken several days to conduct the tests.

Some of those samples had been scraped from the Reeves' home...some were found on articles of clothing...the ax...and bodies.

At the end of his examination, he had concluded, without a doubt, that the blood was human...not animal.

"There was absolutely no guesswork involved with my conclusion," Dr. Butler had assured the court. "My tests are exceedingly accurate."

When Drew had asked the doctor to explain how the tests were conducted, Dr. Butler had cast a skeptical glance towards the jury...as if to size up their ability to comprehend his highly-technical and obviously-important testimony.

He knew he was ahead of his time...and he knew that someday, blood evidence would be highly regarded in courts of law.

"Well, sir, the distinction is between serum and not the blood cells," Dr. Butler had explained. "The cells soon dry up, so we must look at the serum. In making the test, I took specimens of blood from several human beings, Negro and white persons, and also from those of a hog and a rabbit. The blood on the overalls, shoes and shirt was human blood, not blood from an animal."

He said this last statement with finality. He knew no one would dispute such complex testimony from such an expert witness.

Drew was sure that the jury considered the substance found on the shoes in Mark Peters' home to be blood...even if Lunsford wasn't an "expert" witness. Webster Stewart was grasping at the proverbial straw...vainly.

He called his next witness, Ernest Morgan.

If Lunsfords' testimony had sealed Peters coffin...then Ernest Morgan's nailed it shut.

"Mr. Morgan, you were with Mr. Lunsford when a search of the Peters' house was conducted, were you not?"

"Yes, sir, I sure was."

"Do you remember what you found there?"

"Well, sir, we found a pair of blood-stain...er, we found a pair of over-alls that appeared to have blood stains on 'em." Morgan's rephrasing of his sentence drew some chuckles from the court spectators.

"And just where in the defendant's home did you find these overalls?" Drew asked. He was looking at the jury...with his hands outstretched on the banister separating them from the courtroom.

"Well, sir, they was on a clothesline...covered up with some women's clothes."

Drew said nothing for a few seconds...letting the picture of Mark Peters' hanging his bloody clothing on the line and camouflaging them with those of his wife sink in.

"Thank you, Mr. Morgan."

Defense attorney Stewart, thinking the timing might be right, called Mark Peters to the stand next.

The courtroom fell quiet...straining to hear every word the soft-spoken defendant had to say.

****

Mark Peters knew he had disappointed a lot of people, not the least of those being his small son, who thought his daddy "hung the moon."

Passing the hours in jail, his emotions had sauntered from self-pity to anger at the world to resignation of his circumstances.

Why couldn't he have been born white?

Just what kind of God allows his people to be born so different?

Mark didn't know if he believed in God. At the same time, he was scared God would punish him for not believing - so he tried not to think about it at all.

Growing up, he hadn't really thought about equality and fairness much. Heck, the white folks who lived around them didn't have no more than his family did. Everybody worked hard. He had bunches of brothers and sisters. He was the oldest. And his daddy kind of treated him like an equal. It never occurred to him that this was a burden. He just had a natural leadership ability and everyone looked up to him.

When his son was born, things suddenly changed. He began to see things in a new light. He wanted good things for his son. He wanted his son to have more than he had. He wanted his son to live in an equal world.

It was so frustrating.

Mark remembered a conversation he'd had with his friend Chester. They had been talking about the wedding and Chester was saying he hoped he could have a son like he had.

Mark's response had taken Chester by surprise.

"Don't have no god-damned kids," he'd spat out. "Why would you want to raise children in a world that don't treat them equal?"

"So you can love 'em and hope that the world changes...and they can take care of you when you're old," Chester had replied. "What's the matter with you anyway? My mama always said having children was the greatest thing she ever done."

"Your mama is too happy with having nothin'."

Chester took offense.

"She don't see her kids as nothin's. She says the Bible instructs us to have kids...be fruitful and multiply...and raise up the children right."

"Your mama reads the Bible and talks them verses that sound good...but that's all part of some strange people's lives in some way off part of the world. You can't live today like they lived in the Bible."

"Why not?"

"Because!! Things ain't the same today. Hell, just look at us. We supposed to be free. But the Bible talks about slaves and how you gonna treat 'em. What if the Bible was written today? What would it say about slavery? The Bible says everybody is supposed to love everybody and treat people like you want to be treated. And then it tells you how to treat your slaves?"

"Well...that's just it, see. They had slaves back then. Now, we don't have slaves. So, your children will be better off. See?"

"Yeah, I see those folks in town sittin' in their fancy churches and pro'fessin' to love God and Jesus and everybody. And if one of us was to walk in the door, they'd call the sheriff. What I see is, you're a fool if you believe that things are gonna be different for my children - or your children."

"The Bible says you're not supposed to call a man a fool."

"When God tells me how to get the best for my son, I'll start readin' the Bible. 'Til then, it's up to me to see that he gets everything he needs. Jesus ain't gonna do it for me."

Not long after this particular conversation, Mark had started joining the gambling sessions at old man Reeves' place. And when Henry Waller first mentioned robbing the old man...he had listened.

****

Mark's testimony, however, pretty much followed the same lines as his earlier confessions -- with a few exceptions. He said Henry Waller and Johnie Long enticed him to go along to the

Reeves place on the premise that they were going to play cards and drink. He failed to mention the robbery motive.

"If I'd known they was gonna kill them people...I woudna gone," he said.

"Waller and Long the only one's with you?" Stewart asked.

"Chester Tyson, he was with us -- and Larkin Stewart?"

"What about Anderson Heard?"

"No, suh. He wasn't with us."

Monday, January 29, 1917
Webster Parish Courthouse
Minden, Louisiana

The afternoon court session opened with Chester Tyson.

He approached the witness stand on unsteady legs. His knees felt weak...as did his bladder. He was scared...and he wanted to puke.

He had slept fitfully, and had awakened feeling fearful and haunted. He could hazily remember having one of those nightmares where something unworldly was chasing him through a dark pit - not unlike how he envisioned Hell.

He didn't know what his pursuer was, but it was evil. He didn't want to get too close a look, not even in a dream, because its aura stank of maggots and rot. Just as the being got close enough to reach out and touch Chester with a fleshless hand, he was startled awake. He lay in his dark cell sweating, heart pumping...still terrified and afraid to open his eyes. He imagined the putrid smell still clinging to his nostrils.

The dream had lingered, and as he stepped up to take his seat in the witness box he was suddenly overwhelmed by a feeling of doom...and helplessness. Horrible, horrible helplessness. And guilt.

Married less than a day, Chester had been carted off to jail and accused of murdering a white family. And all 'cause of that crazy white bastard.

Of course, either way he was a dead man. The white jury was gonna hang him for sure. But if he had refused to go along....Henry woulda killed him. He had no doubt of that. Henry was crazy like no man he'd ever known.

He remembered how crazy Henry looked the night when he came and got him to go over to the Reeves.

It was well after midnight.

Anderson was sleepin' over. They'd celebrated his upcoming weddin' a little too much. Bootleg whiskey will kick a man's ass faster than a red neck boss man. Fact was, he was still feelin' the effects of bad booze when Henry knocked on the door.

It was a light knock, but Chester'd heard it. He'd been lying awake listening to Anderson snore...thinkin' about Josephine and worrying about the weddin'...and how he was gonna get enough money to make a decent life for a wife and family.

"Come on Chester, get your goddamned clothes on, we're going over to old man Reeves' place."

Henry's squinty eyes had that sinister look...the look they always had when he'd had too much to drink and was lookin' for trouble. He was carrying a shotgun...but that wasn't unusual. He was often armed. And Chester seriously believed that years of drinkin' bad liquor had twisted Henry's mind. He was rarely sober, 'specially since his wife had died.

"Mr. Henry, I'd better pass," Chester remembered saying. "I'm none too sober and tomorrow's a big day for me...I prob'ly need to get some sleep."

"Look, nigger," Waller leaned in toward Chester, tapping his shoulder blade with the shotgun -- he could smell stale liquor on his breath. "You're gonna get your ass in gear and come with me to Reeves'. I need some more liquor and I feel lucky tonight, you know what I mean? And you need all the luck you can get...cause you ain't gonna get no black pussy, married or not, if you ain't got no money."

Henry waited on the porch while Chester threw a pair of overalls over his long-johns, slipped his feet into cold, damp shoes, and grabbed his coat. He was careful not to awaken his sleeping mother.

"You got an ax...might need an ax to cut some pine saplings," Waller said when Chester stepped out the door. Scared of asking too many more questions, Chester rescued an ax from the woodpile.

Henry took it from Chester and held it up in front of him.

"Yeah, looks like a pretty good ax."

His smile was cold.

"Let's go."

They'd just about reached Mark's house when Chester saw what he thought was an apparition in the middle of the road. It turned out to be that strange white boy, Johnie Long. Chester wondered if the boy had been "persuaded" to come along in the same manner he had.

The three of them awakened Mark. His friend, Larkin Stewart, had also slept over. Chester recalled that neither man wanted to join them. But true to his nature, Henry wouldn't take "no" for an answer.

The minute they reached the Reeves house, Chester knew something was wrong. Only one light was on. It looked like the family had already turned in.

"You used to work for the old man....call him out here," Henry told Chester. They were standing a few feet from the porch and Henry was talking just above a whisper.

"They's all in bed," Chester remembered replying.

"Goddamn it," Waller snarled, starting up the steps. "Come on Johnie boy, we'll wake him up."

Johnie, Mark and Larkin climbed the steps also. Chester remained planted in the yard. Henry called out Reeves' name and gently pushed on the door with the ax. When it creaked open, Chester couldn't tell if someone, perhaps a child, had heard Henry's call...or if it was merely the force of Henry's push that did it.

Henry turned back to them.

"If that bastard runs out, you stop him, you hear me?"

Waller, Johnie and Mark stepped into the sleeping house.

Larkin bounded off the porch and joined Chester in the yard "standing guard" at a safe distance. They waited and watched.

When the hurt scream of a child pierced the thick silence, Chester and Larkin looked at each other. Chester could see Lark's temples pulsing...the urge to take flight was strong.

Suddenly Mark came tearing through the door. He flung himself down the steps, fell to his knees, and vomited.

Before they could question him, a terrified woman came bursting through the door in her bare feet, with Henry in pursuit, brandishing the ax like a Medicine Show Indian with a tomahawk.

The ax was crimson.

Henry had just managed to grab the hem of her dress when they disappeared around the side of the house. Chester could only imagine what happened next when he heard several sloppy thuds. He knew the sound well. His own mother made it when she whacked the heads off chickens before she fried them.

...She even used the same ax.

Chester remembered freezing...his feet felt planted in the yard. He had at once felt simultaneously cold...and hot...like the time he unwittingly touched a frayed spot on the lamp cord in Mr.

57

Will's hardware store. Mr. Will said he'd been shocked. All he knew was he never wanted it to happen again.

Then Henry was on the porch barking orders.

"Chester."

He jumped.

"Get on in there and fetch the old man's money chest -- you know the one, you've seen him make change from it a thousand times."

The last place Chester wanted to go was in that house. But the last person he wanted to cross was Henry Waller. He stepped over the threshold.

From the glow of the fireplace, Chester made out the form of Johnie Long. He stood frozen in the middle of a blood-splattered room. He jumped, startled, when Chester came in. For a moment, their eyes locked. Then the boy ran out, leavin' Chester to find the chest and drag it outside, which he did.

Mark forced open the lock and was pushed aside by Waller before he could open the creaky lid. Chester couldn't see what, if anything, Henry removed from it.

"Boys we haven't got much time," Henry said, straightening up. His speech was breathy. As he talked he wiped blood from his hands on an old rag he'd found on the porch. You'd have thought it was something he did every day. He tossed it aside without another thought.

"Whew wee, we've really played the devil here tonight. But we gotta get outta here...Chester, you take this pistol," he thrust a gun into his hand. "Everybody knows you've got one and they won't question you. If any of you do get questioned...you better not say a word...'Cause if you do, I'll kill you -- I proved it tonight. I'll kill you if it takes me 40 years to do it."

****

The courtroom had grown quiet when Chester began speaking, his voice low, his words soft.

Now he was finished, and he felt better than he had in a long time.

He hadn't wanted to testify, until Mr. Stewart pointed out that, even if he couldn't save himself, perhaps his telling the story to the jury would convince them of his friend Anderson's innocence. Now that he had done that, he felt pretty much at peace.

After all, he had gone along with Waller.

And he had to admit, if just to himself, that it should have been pretty obvious Henry wasn't goin' to old man Reeves' to play cards and get liquored up and have a good time. Admittedly, it was one thing to reckon with Henry when he was sober, and quite another when he was drunk. Henry'd been drunk when he came to his house that night. And he wasn't in no mood to take "no" for an answer.

Of course murder was somethin' else...but he had been there and he hadn't done nothin' to help those people...not even the children.

Guess he deserved what was comin' to him.

But if Henry got away with murder....he'd see him in hell.

****

Judge Sandlin was hoping to end the trial in a single day. All-in-all they were making pretty good progress. Since 10 o'clock that morning, they had seated a jury and heard the testimony of dozens of witnesses.

He had been worried about a speedy trial when Stewart subpoenaed 29 witnesses early on. Not to be outdone, Drew had turned around and ordered 31 to appear in court for the State.

How they managed to keep the trial a secret with that many people involved was a mystery to him. Early that morning, Tyson, Peters, and Stewart had been chained together, placed on the V.S.&P. train in Shreveport and transported to Sibley. At the Sibley depot, they had been transferred into a waiting car by deputies and brought to the Webster Parish Courthouse, where they were fed breakfast in jail along with Anderson Heard. Maybe the earliness of the hour helped. He didn't know.

But secrecy had been important. Judge Sandlin wasn't going to risk having people mob the courthouse just to get seats for the trial of the century. No, sir.

Of course, word gradually leaked out and people began drifting in to the courtroom. After all the seats were filled, no one else was allowed to enter.

Thank God the defense attorney had chosen to focus his energy on saving Heard's neck...pretty much sacrificing Tyson and Peters.

Judge Sandlin knew this wasn't exactly right...but given the two men's confessions, they'd about sealed their own fates before the trial even began. Larkin Stewart's fate would probably be a toss up.

Of course, the jury could see things differently -- all four Negroes might hang...it just all depended on how benevolent the jury was feeling.

It was now 10:30 p.m. Time for closing arguments. If luck was with them, they'd have a verdict before midnight.

****

"Gentlemen, the hour is late and I'll not take much more of your time."

Harmon Drew directed his comments to the 12 white men who were seated in the jury box to his right.

It had taken only two hours that morning to seat them. And much of that time had been consumed by Defense Attorney Stewart's attempts to determine the effects of pre-trial publicity on his case. Drew had been patient with Stewart's berating of the press, since he too was a rapid opponent of pre-trial publicity.

"There should be a law against publishing what purports to be the facts in a criminal case before it has been tried and disposed of," Drew had acrimoniously stated during a brief break, loudly enough to be heard by reporters covering the trial.

During the jury selection process, Drew and assistant DA Thomas W. Robertson had focused their efforts on finding jurors they perceived as educated enough to listen intelligently, and bold enough to ask questions about points of law they did not understand.

This always lessened the chances for a defense attorney's successful appeal of the case to a higher court.

The results were a jury of eight farmers of seemingly above-average intelligence, a grocer, a clerk, a merchant, and a patent medicine salesman. The men either lived or conducted business in the nearby villages of Yellowpine, Sibley, Heflin, Leton, Sibley, Shongaloo, Doyline, and McIntyre. The court's strong opposition to having anyone serve who was too familiar with the case virtually eliminated citizens from Minden, where the newspapers were more widely distributed and consumed.

John J. Slack, a clerk from Shongaloo, was elected to serve as jury foreman.

Drew had kept his eye on the jurors throughout the day and he perceived that they were attentive...and had listened to the facts.

That's why his final remarks could be brief.

As it was, Stewart's closing argument more or less took the form of a plea for the lives of Anderson Heard and Larkin Stewart.

"I beseech you to consider the mental capacity of my client, Anderson Heard. He is a simple-minded boy. Does his incompetence warrant the death penalty? I think not. You've heard at least one witness claim that he wasn't present at the murders. And by omission during other testimony, you must deduce that he wasn't. As for my client, Larkin Stewart...his presence at the murder scene is at least questionable. I ask you to spare his neck in the name of justice...in the name of all that is fair."

"As for Chester Tyson and Mark Peters...were they not dupes of a far more intelligent and scheming man?"

"Objection. No one else is on trial here," Drew pointed out.

"Sustained."

"Yes, they admitted being there," Stewart continued, non-plussed. "But please consider their fear...the fear they had of a man whose reputation for ill-will is well-known in this community."

"Objection, who is on trial, your honor?" Drew couldn't believe Stewart was continuing, even in closing.

"True, that man is not on trial here," Stewart said, before Judge Sandlin could reply. "But his reputation has certainly preceded him into this courtroom. Will you not spare my clients...especially Mr. Heard and Mr. Stewart? I beseech you to spare their lives..."

Stewart returned to his seat.

Leaving Harmon Drew one last parting shot.

"You know all the facts," Drew said. "You've heard all the evidence. I don't ask you to break Anderson Heard's neck. My respected opponent is right -- he was made a dupe. But shouldn't he be put away? Should we leave one conspirator free to move among respected society? I think not."

"Five people are dead....Three young children were butchered...murdered in their beds as they slept the sleep of the innocent...dreaming about a Christmas morning they would never see. Who is going to pay for three lost little lives? For a loving mother? For a proud father? Who?"

"That's for you to decide, gentlemen. And God be with you while you do."

Tuesday, January 30, 1917
Webster Parish Courthouse
Minden, Louisiana

It was 12:03 a.m.

Deputies stationed in the courthouse hallway looked relieved when the door to the sequestering room opened and the jury foreman stepped out.

After all, it had been nearly an hour...and a quick verdict had been expected.

"Beg your pardon, son, we've got a question for the judge," Slack said to the nearest deputy.

"Yes, sir, Mr. Slack, I'll go tell him."

The wearied young law officer couldn't mask his disappointment. He had promised his wife a special dinner tonight...last night to be more precise, since it was now after midnight. It was their second anniversary...and to commemorate it, she'd told him they could start working on a family. Now, not only did she miss a night out on the town...he sure wasn't going to get his gift either. She'd be in no mood.

He could sure use some diapepsin.

****

Sheriff Phillips couldn't believe no one had left the courtroom. This, despite the fact that tomorrow -- today, actually -- was an ordinary work day.

He'd figured that, as the day wore on, the crowd would start taking advantage of recesses and slip out. He'd been wrong.

When the jury left the room at 11:50 to begin deliberations, the crowd remained.

"Hey, Sheriff, why don't you let 'em stand up so's we all can see 'em," somebody in the back of the room yelled.

The defendants had been sitting quietly for the most part. A few members of the press had begun leaning over the railing, asking questions. They hadn't seemed to mind, so he hadn't objected.

"Do you fellas mind standing so the people in the back can see you?" Sheriff Phillips asked it as a question, but as he did so, he motioned for the four to rise. They did.

Mark Peters clutched a sweat-stained hat that was probably once black, but was now a faded gray, most probably a hand-me-down from some white farmer. He stared hard at it in his hands as if he expected it to sprout wings and fly any second. He maintained his dignity while feeling like an animal at a livestock show.

Larkin Stewart pulled on a cigarette. He seemed more approachable, and stared into the crowd.

"Hey, Larkin, tell us the truth. Were you there or not?" a small balding man poised with pad and pen asked, taking advantage of Stewart's apparent willingness to accept the spectators for what they were -- merely curious onlookers -- not hostile whites bent on seeing a negra hang.

"No, suh, I wasn' there," Stewart mumbled, looking sideways. "And I didn't know nothin' 'bout them killin's...did'n have nuthin' to do with it."

Tyson answered the reporters' questions just as he had on the stand. There would be no new revelations while the jury was locked in debate. While he stood close to the railing, he looked sideways for the most part, avoiding direct eye contact with anyone. He knew the pecking order, and although the crowd was respectful enough, he knew he was in a white man's court.

Heard stood dumbly looking down. He made no effort to speak or look at the crowd -- and no one asked him anything.

The deputy's sudden appearance in the doorway motioning for Sheriff Phillips had sent people scattering for their seats like mice playing musical chairs, anxious for a verdict. The jury was then escorted back into the courtroom.

"Gentlemen, I understand you have a question," Judge Sandlin asked, once the jury was seated. The disappointment of the crowd was audible, and the judge lightly tapped his gavel.

Twelve pairs of eyes trained themselves on his honor.

"Yes, sir," Slack respectfully came to his feet. "We're pretty divided here, mainly 'cause we feel like...if we find these four negras guilty of murder...they won't be able to convict the ringleader behind this thing. And we're pretty much agreed that the man responsible for this crime ain't on trial today. We really need some advice on how to proceed. Could you explain to us again how to write up a verdict?"

As Slack bumbled recklessly into his speech, Judge Sandlin flushed and sat bolt upright...but it was too late to shut him up. He should have met with the jury in private...not in open court so all the world could hear. He should have instructed the jury to disregard Webster Stewart's prejudicial remarks about an unindicted suspect. Not that it would have made a difference, but he should have done it anyway.

He motioned for the jury foreman and both attorneys to approach the bench. When they were all assembled out of earshot of the crowd, he leaned forward.

"Just how split are you, Mr. Slack?" the judge asked, not bothering to mask his annoyance. Webster Stewart had the good manners to look sheepish for Slack's sake. Drew had noticed the reporters writing like crazy as Slack was talking and already he was worried about the State's chances of getting a conviction in the next trial. He could see the headlines now - "Jury Ready to Convict Unindicted Suspect."

Only Slack was unaware of the trouble his disclosure of jury deliberations could cause.

"Well, sir, as it stands right now, we got eight who wanna find all four negras guilty of manslaughter or guilty without capital punishment...other four are leanin' towards guilty as charged."

"You do know that a verdict of guilty, as charged in this case, carries an automatic penalty of death?" Judge Sandlin asked.

"Yes, sir, I think we're all aware of that. But would that make a difference when it comes to the next trial?"

"Let me digress here, Mr. Slack, and repeat some earlier instructions to you...perhaps you didn't quite understand...I know the trial process is somewhat complicated...and a capital murder case always is...There are four verdicts that you can return -- guilty as charged, guilty without capital punishment, guilty of manslaughter, or not guilty -- which is an acquittal. I think the problem lies in the fact that you are trying to convict all four defendants equally. But you don't have to do that. Any one of the four verdicts can apply to any one...or two...or all....of the defendants."

"And as to the matter of the next trial...believe me, gentlemen, guilty verdicts here...or, on the other hand, any verdicts rendered here today should in no way affect the outcome of another trial. And, Mr. Slack, that's if there is another trial."

At 1 a.m., after ascertaining that a verdict was nowhere near, Judge Sandlin ordered the jury to take a rest. He instructed them to resume deliberating at precisely 8 o'clock.

Cuffed and manacled, Tyson, Peters, Heard, and Stewart were returned to their cells.

The disbursement of justice would have to wait a few more hours.

One by one the jurors filed back into the courtroom. Somewhat refreshed, with welcome daylight filtering through the dusty venetian blinds, it had taken them only an hour to reach the decisions that had seemed so elusive eight hours earlier.

E.M. Barton, Sid Harris, E.E. Heflin, A.T. Lee, G.I. Herren, G.G. Kirkpatrick, H.R. Griffith, and E.A. Woods were all farmers. Henry Tillman was a merchant. R.S. Barrington sold patent medicines. D.S. Davis was a grocer, and jury foreman Slack was a clerk. Right now they all had one thing in common -- the fates of four Negroes charged in the most heinous crime of the century.

"Gentlemen, have you reached your verdicts?"

The standing-room only crowd got dead quiet as Judge Sandlin spoke.

"Yes, we have, your honor," Slack stood, holding several pieces of paper in his hand.

"Would you give those to Clerk McKinney," the judge instructed.

"Defendants, you may rise."

Slowly and deliberately, the four men got to their feet. They stood expressionless, looking at Judge Sandlin.

"Mr. McKinney would you read the verdicts."

Second Judicial District Court Clerk Will McKinney cleared his throat.

"In the matter of the State of Louisiana versus Anderson Heard and Larkin Stewart, we, the jury, find the defendants guilty as charged without capital punishment."

A low mumbling issued from the spectators...heads nodded in agreement. It was obvious what the next verdicts would be.

"In the matter of the State of Louisiana versus Mark Peters and Chester Tyson, we, the jury, find the defendants guilty as charged."

****

Sheriff Phillips had always made a habit of watching a defendant's face as a verdict was read. Many times, for him at least, the whole guilt and innocence thing came down to that fleeting portion of a second when the verdict was pronounced. There were different looks that defendants gave. If a man was guilty and was found guilty, you could read it in his eyes. If he was guilty and was found innocent, it was there, the spark of triumph. If he was innocent and was found guilty, thank God that rarely happened, there was this look of sheer terror and desperation.

There was nothing he could read in the eyes of these defendants. The spectators had reacted more strongly. They just stood there, stoic, unaffected.

"Mr. Tyson, Mr. Peters, you may sit down. Mr. Heard and Mr. Stewart, remain standing." Judge Sandlin rustled a stack of papers on his desk, and looked over the top of his spectacles at the defendants.

"Is there anything that you have to say as to why the sentence of the Law should not be pronounced against you?"

The defendants shook their heads

"No, suh," Stewart managed.

The judge proceeded.

"By reason of a bill of indictment charging defendants Anderson Heard and Larkin Stewart with murder, and their conviction by a jury of guilty as charged without capital punishment, it is ordered, adjudged and decreed that Anderson Heard and Larkin Stewart, the defendants for said crime, be confined at hard labor in the Louisiana State Penitentiary for a period of their natural lives."

Pencil leads raced across reporters' pads.

"You may sit down....Mr. Peters, Mr. Tyson will you stand."

"Is there anything that you have to say as to why the sentence of the Law should not be pronounced against you?"

"No, suh."

"No, suh."

"By reason of the law and the evidence being in favor of the State and against you, and by further reason of the indictment and endorsements thereon, and considering the verdict of the jury finding you guilty of murder as charged, it is ordered, adjudged, and decreed that you, Mark Peters and Chester Tyson, be hanged by the neck until you are dead."

"You will be remanded into the hands of the sheriff for transfer to the State Penitentiary to await your executions. The dates will be fixed by the Governor."

"This court is adjourned."

****

"Hey, Sheriff, let us snap a picture...come on just one picture."

The reporters were lined up behind the railing, shouting questions and asking for photos.

"Okay, boys, I'll give you 15 minutes. I got to have my prisoners on the L&A when it pulls out at 11:45 so make it fast. You can ask a few questions and take one picture. I'll have 'em sit for you."

Sheriff Phillips motioned for a deputy to line up four chairs about four feet behind the railing. Then he seated the convicted men and opened the floor up for questions.

When a photographer's bulb exploded, startling them, they all four laughed, seeming at ease now that the trial was over -- not giving a conscious thought to what awaited them.

"Is there any testimony that you would change?" a reporter from the *Shreveport Journal* asked.

Mark Peters studied him a second.

"I was in the house," he finally said. "I was standin' at the foot of the old man's bed when he was killed - that's how the blood got on my shirt. But soon's I saw what was happenin', I runned out of the house. I didn't go there to kill nobody and I didn't kill nobody. 'Specially them babies."

"Do you think you got a fair trial?"

Blank stares.

"Mark, do you think you got a fair trial?"

Peters hesitated.

"Yeah, I guess so. They give us a fair trial, I reckon. It's what I was expectin'. But I don't think they ought to hang us. And they sure ought not to send Anderson to jail for the rest of his life - - he wasn't even there."

Wednesday, January 31, 1917
Main Street
Minden, Louisiana

"Think they got a fair trial, sir?"

Newspaper reporter William Harper paused in front of the Bank of Minden. He and his boss had just left the Webster Parish Courthouse and were making their way to the *Webster Signal* office. He made a pretense of studying the intricate green mosaic tiles adorning the bank's entrance as he waited for an answer.

Thomas W. Fuller, owner and editor of Minden's weekly newspaper, cast him a fatherly look.

"I think they were involved, if that's what you mean...After all, they admitted being there, didn't they?"

He shrugged and began to walk again.

"Admitting you were there, and deserving to hang, are two different things. Just look at the circumstances. I mean, these guys weren't exactly geniuses, and they were scared of Waller. On top of that, you've got three of 'em telling the world that the fourth one wasn't even there. And you've got the conflicting stories...Every time they talked to a different deputy, they told a different story. Okay, so Chester Tyson and Mark Peters both admitted - during the trial - that they were there. But Heard and Stewart both repudiated their earlier confessions."

Getting no response, the young reporter continued.

"And how do you suppose Sheriff Phillips managed to empanel a jury so quickly? Weren't you surprised at how the sheriff managed to root out so many people who had no interest in the murder and knew so little about it -- at least that they admitted knowing."

He said it more as a statement than a question.

"I mean, come on, this was the biggest thing since Jack the Ripper -- and old Jack probably got less attention from the press. At least Jack the Ripper apparently wasn't a negra -- so he'd probably have received a fairer trial. Those jurors had their minds made up going in."

With that, Thomas Fuller held up his hands, signaling that he'd heard enough.

"Son, you know this was not a racial thing, so don't go trying to make it one. You know good and well why it took that

68

jury so long to come to a decision. A majority of them felt like if the Negroes were convicted of murder, it would be impossible to return a verdict of guilty against Henry Waller -- and that's who, you well know, they think was behind the whole thing. You keep in mind that the next two fellas to stand trial are white, and well-to-do, for that matter. I believe in the system. And I think justice will be served."

"We'll see, sir, we'll see."

PART II

Friday, January 12, 1917
Rapides Parish Jail
Alexandria, Louisiana

"Hey, Waller, you intrested in readin' the newspaper?"

The abrasive voice reached him from the bunk above his head. Its owner was a nasty-looking middle-aged man who had a perpetual dribble of brown tobacco juice seeping from the side of his mouth, stained underarms, and a smell to match both.

He could hear him rustling the pages of what was probably a days-old newspaper sent to him by some even crazier family member.

"You know I ain't interested in reading an old newspaper. Why? You think I've got a stake in the price of cotton or something?" Henry Waller despised his cellmate, and was looking forward to the day he no longer had to share this cramped, smelly hole with him.

He'd calmed down considerably since his initial arrest, when all he could think about was being seized by an angry mob of men bent an hangin' him as a baby killer. He knew it had happened before - and it could happen again.

But the niggers had been convicted. And that had lessened his anxiety level somewhat.

He also knew that Sheriff Hughes of Caddo Parish was inclined to believe Johnie Long and the niggers had framed him. Now if Hughes could just convince the grand jury, he'd be a free man.

It was a good thing he'd been in Sarepta that night visiting relatives -- relatives who were willing to support his story.

God, he needed a drink.

His cellmate was obnoxiously persistent.

"Ah hum, let me read ya this...let's see, 'The Webster Parish Grand Jury, in presentin' its final report here this mornin', returned four bills for murder 'ginst Henry Waller, farmer, and Johnie Long, both white men, charged with com, charged with com, comp...'"

"Give me that god-damned newspaper," Waller swore and jumped from his bunk, grabbing the *Journal* from his cellmate's crusty hands.

"....charged with complicity in the killing of five members of the family of John Nelson Reeves Christmas eve night," he steadied himself against the bars and read silently.

Why hadn't he been told?

"Waller and Long are both in custody. Warrants will be served upon them either today or tomorrow and a date will be set for their trial. It is not likely that this date will be announced in advance. The authorities are likely to follow the same policy pursued in the case of the four Negroes recently tried for participation in the Reeves tragedy and convicted."

"However, it is not possible to try the accused men immediately. The jury has been discharged by District Judge John N. Sandlin and next week that official will hold court in Bossier Parish. The next criminal term will not begin in Webster Parish until Feb. 26. Waller and Long will probably be arraigned on that date."

"It is expected that there will be a warm fight over the Waller and Long case when it is called to trial. Waller, in particular, was a man of influence in his section of the parish and has numerous friends and relatives. An effort will be made to establish alibis for both men. It is not known whether the Negroes, recently convicted, will be brought from the penitentiary to testify, but they probably will..."

Waller threw the paper in the direction of his cellmate and swore.

"Damned right I'm a man of influence...bastards think they're gonna convict me...they got another thing comin'...god-damn it...treatin' me like I was one of them niggers. And if any piss-poor lawyer thinks he can get any one of them boys to look me in the eye and say I did it, he's got another thing comin'..."

"Damn it, I could use a drink of whiskey!"

Having dodged the airborne newspaper, Henry Waller's cellmate made a show of prissily rearranging it. He used the back of his hand to wipe a stream of mohagony-colored tobacco spittle from his chin.

"By the way, Mr. Influence...," he snickered, "Did you notice the price of cotton fell 31 cents a pound last night?"

On Wednesday, February 27, Sheriff Phillips slipped Henry Waller out of the Rapides Parish Jail and escorted him to Minden, where he was formally arraigned.

Two reputable men of the bar had been engaged by Waller's family to handle the case—Thomas Webster Robertson, a Minden attorney and former assistant District Attorney for Bossier/Webster Parishes; and former District Judge William C. Barnette, who at one time had served as special counsel to the Caddo Parish District Attorney and was former district judge and prosecutor for Bienville Parish.

They would be going against two of the State's best—Bossier/Webster District Attorney Harmon Drew and his assistant, former Caddo Parish DA James M. Foster. Drew was none-to-pleased that Robertson had agreed to represent Waller, since he had co-prosecuted the earlier case against the Negroes. This was an all-too-common practice and not one that sat well with Drew.

The defense team entered a plea of not guilty to murder. Trial was set for March 12. Until that time, Waller would be incarcerated in the Caddo Parish Jail in Shreveport.

Johnie Long was not arraigned—a sure sign that he would be used as a witness in the case against his former boss and friend. He had, through his father, obtained the services of a Shreveport attorney, Frank E. Blanchard.

No one knew for sure, but it was assumed that the four convicted Negroes would be brought from the Louisiana State Penitentiary at Angola to testify.

In the meantime, the Grove citizens, now calling themselves the "Organization to Suppress All Lawlessness," were hard at work.

They had composed and sent to the *Webster Signal* a second set of resolutions, which the newspaper had printed verbatim.

"Whereas there has been recently committed in our community one of the most horrible murders; and Whereas there is more or less gambling in our neighborhood," the statement read, "We desire to express to the world, first, our disapproval of the commission of crimes of all kinds, and second, that we are sorry to state that some of our citizens have been gambling and drinking; committing various unlawful and unusual acts which we condemn.

We hereby pledge ourselves to do our best to rid our community of all whiskey-selling, gambling, and the commission of all other crimes and immoral acts; that we forbid all persons from committing any said acts on our premises; and in case we know of the law being violated will report said violators to the officers and the grand jury of Webster Parish."

The "Organization to Suppress All Lawlessness" would be permanent, the communication revealed.

It was signed by Luke M. Grigsby and Will Sexton.

Monday, March 12, 1917
Webster Parish Courthouse
Minden, Louisiana

"Bailiff, instruct Sheriff Phillips to lock the doors to the courthouse so that no one else can enter unless they state their business."

Judge Sandlin was annoyed - at least to the extent that he allowed himself to become annoyed. He was, by nature, a calm, tolerant man.

But jury selection hadn't even begun and already spectators were spilling out onto the brick courtyard. One would think the notorious Pancho Villa had been apprehended in their midst and was being tried right here in his court.

No, he wasn't going to allow spectators to disrespect his courtroom. He was already bending his own rules to allow people to stand in the halls. If they wanted to stay, they had better mind their manners and keep still.

The selection of jurors would empty some seats, but not many. Those who were potential jurors would probably opt to stay...despite the fact that it was planting season for most. But the cotton and row crops could wait...at least for one more day.

Judge Sandlin reflected.

The whole world appeared to be waiting.

The "Black Tom" explosion at that U.S. munitions dock in New Jersey had been traced to German saboteurs. It probably wouldn't be too long before the U.S. entered the War. How many of the fresh young boys in this crowd, he wondered, will be shipped off to some lonely, foreign country to fight a war they didn't start...never to return.

He thought of his own 17-year-old son, Nicholas. He couldn't bear the thought of him dying in some God-forbidden foreign land. He was the only child he had. He had lost his wife and his newborn daughter, Ruth, shortly after taking the oath of office as judge for the 2nd Judicial District Court in March of 1911.

He loved his country. But he was not willing to sacrifice his only child.

By 1 o'clock, only four jurors had been seated—W.B.F. Holt, H.P. Hodges, Ellis H. Miller, and C.W. Whitaker. They were chosen from the regular panel. All the others had been eliminated by Drew or Robertson.

The rest would have to be selected from an extra venire of 100 citizens ordered drawn up by Judge Sandlin.

He adjourned court until 10 the following morning.

Tuesday, March 13, 1917
Webster Parish Courthouse
Minden, Louisiana

Jury selection Tuesday proceeded more swiftly, requiring only a couple of hours to seat the final eight members.

Only one juror admitted to not having read anything about the case - Tom Wilkerson, who lived very close to the Bossier Parish line. Every other juror - J.M. Culverhouse, T. J. Turner, J.E. Farrar, W. A. Gray, Jim Murrell, W. G. Burford, and C.U. Jones - admitted to hearing or reading something about the murders. However, all 12 professed to having formed no opinion.

Judge Sandlin recessed court until 1:30 that afternoon. Again, ever vigilant, he ordered the courthouse doors locked, and everyone entering was to be searched by his special squad of newly-sworn volunteer deputies.

To anyone's knowledge, no threats had been made against Waller - probably out of respect to the family. Still, the ever-vigilant judge had ordered around-the-clock security for the defendant.

As in the trial of the Negroes, his honor refused to allow people to occupy the side aisles in the courtroom. Standing was only allowed in the rear.

Many people were disappointed over not being allowed in the courthouse after coming from as far as 40 miles away by wagon, motor car, or train. Instead, they were forced to loiter in the halls outside the second floor courtroom straining for a random word or two. Others gathered outside in the courtyard.

The cafes and shops in the area were doing a brisk business, as were the town liveries and jitney drivers.

When court adjourned that afternoon, not a seat stood empty. Those spectators jammed into the rear of the room stood shoulder-to-shoulder. Fortunately for them, Louisiana's sweltering summer was still a few months away.

Many of those seated in the courtroom were related either to the victims or the defendant, or were considered witnesses, or both.

Sharing the defense table with Waller and his attorneys were the defendant's brothers, Jesse Waller of Sarepta and Dr. L.T.

Waller of Como, Texas; his brother-in-law, Walter W. Dean, also of Sarepta; and Judge Coyle.

****

Cody Reeves, wide-eyed with curiosity and obviously enjoying the attention of so many adults, was the first witness to take the stand for the State.

People found it hard to imagine what this young slip of a boy must have felt when he found his father dead and his brothers butchered.

He was small for a seven-year-old. His sun-bleached hair and tanned complexion testified to his love for the outdoors, where he had spent countless hours playing hide-and-seek, kick the can, and baseball with his brothers and neighboring children. His translucent blue eyes occasionally reflected curiosity at the interest being shown in him. Whether he was talking or listening, his small, delicate mouth formed a slight perpetual smile.

He was accompanied by his much-older half-brother, Charles Reeves of Hortman, with whom he'd gone to live after the deaths of his parents and brothers. Four other half-brothers, J.N. Reeves, R.B. Reeves, J.M. Reeves, and G.I. Reeves, all lived in Texas and were unable to come.

"Cody, we want you to help us find out who killed your mommy and daddy, and brothers."

Assistant DA James M. Foster stood to the little boy's side, looked out at the spectators, and swept the room with his hand

"David was your big brother wasn't he?" Foster asked.

"Yes, sir. He was nine. But Woodrow and Alto was both younger 'n me...I was their big brother..."

"That's right...your baby brother Alto was just 15 months old, wasn't he?"

"Yes, sir, that's right. But he'd be 17 months old now if he'd 'a lived."

Foster smiled and nodded. He had intended, via this line of questioning, to win the hearts of the jury early on...and the little boy's last statement was certainly heart-wrenching.

"Cody, some people have said that you were sleeping in the loft on Christmas eve night when the bad people broke into your house, do you remember?"

"No, sir, I wasn't sleepin' in the loft...cause it was too cold. I was sleepin' in my bed. Mama had throwed some wash over

77

there...so I just climbed in under the wash..." He hesitated. "Mama didn't mind though..."

"I'm sure she didn't, Cody." Foster paused long enough for the jury to take note of several ladies in the crowd dabbing their eyes. "Can you tell us about what time it was when you went to bed?"

"I don't rightly know...it was a good time after dark. Pa'd come home and told us we'd better get to bed early cause Santa Claus was acomin' - and he wouldn't stop by our house if we wasn't asleep. Mama usually made us go to bed 'round nine...cause 'a havin' to go to school the next day. But bein' as we didn't hafta go to school, we got to stay up longer. But I don't rightly know what time it was. Pa went to bed a pretty good time after we did..he was snorin' real loud. Mama was out in the kitchen for a pretty good while...That's all I 'member."

"Do you remember waking up?"

"Well....I remember bein' scared awake 'cause I heard a noise. But I just closed my eyes real tight and listened, and then I didn' hear nothin' else. I didn' want Santa Claus to think I wasn't sleepin'...Then, I musta fell asleep again, 'cause I woke up and the sun was near to comin' up. I got out'ta bed to go find David so we could see what Santa Claus brung us."

"Will it upset you to tell us some more, Cody?" Foster knew the boy was too young to truly understand the nature of what he had seen. But he didn't want to push him and have the jury think him unfeeling.

"I can tell you some more if'n you want me to."

"Okay."

"It was kinda dark and I couldn't find nobody at first. Then I found David - he was kinda layin' on the kitchen floor holding onto Alto. Both of 'em had blood all over 'em...it scared me real bad...cause I didn't know what happened. I tried to get David to get up, but he couldn't...he was tryin' to whisper somethin' to me, but I couldn't understand him...so I told him I'd go fetch Pa. But when I got close to Pa's bed I stepped in somethin' that felt real icky...and Pa wouldn't answer me, so I ran to look for Mama."

"Were you scared, Cody?"

"Yes, sir. I started cryin'...'cause I couldn't find Mama. Then I 'bout stumbled over Woodrow on the floor. And he

78

wouldn't wake up...no matter how hard I shook him...and his head was all bashed in."

"So you decided to go get help, didn't you?"

"Yes, sir. I was real scared so I went on down to fetch Mr. Braselton. I don't cry lots, you know...cause David always calls me a sissy when I cry..."

For a moment the youth look bewildered.

"You're not a sissy, Cody, you're a real brave boy," Foster said, walking over to the defense table. He picked up a pair of baby shoes.

"Were these your baby brother's shoes, Cody?" The tiny shoes dangled from his hand, well in view of the jury box.

"Objection, your honor," Barnette was on his feet.

"Your honor, I am just trying to show the jury the age of the infant killed." Foster figured he had overstepped his bounds, but he had made his point.

He was right.

"I'm going to sustain the objection, counselor. I think this child has testified long enough."

****

J. W. Braselton, Grady Braselton, W. L. Smith, and Jewel Johnson followed Cody on the stand, each pretty much substantiating Cody's story and elaborating in regard to the parts they played in the discovery of the crime.

At 2:20, the State called Johnie L. Long.

Johnie's normally close-cropped hair fell unevenly around his ears and collar, giving him an unkempt look despite his clean-shaven face. His 5',10" 160-pound frame, once boyishly lanky, was now thin. His skin had taken on a sallow look, and void of the sun's bleaching rays, his hair had reverted to its natural brown.

Drew opened questioning with the usual formalities.

In December of 1916, the witness was living on the Waller place in Germantown with his sister, Eva Anderson. He worked for Waller doing odd jobs. Waller had only recently moved into the house in Germantown, having lived in Grove until a few weeks prior to his arrest.

On Christmas eve, he and Eva had traveled the ten miles to their parents' home in Evergreen. That afternoon, they visited his brother, Jim, who lived a short distance away. He attended the wedding of Mike Martin at the Kirkley place later that evening, then returned to his father's and stepmother's house, where everyone had retired at about 11 o'clock.

His parents' house was what you call a "double pen" or "dog trot" made of pine logs, with a long hallway dividing the two sides. When he discovered his Pa had locked the door to the room he and his stepbrother were sharing, he tried a window, but made too much noise, so he removed some logs leading into the hall and slipped out that way.

"And what time was that?" Drew asked.

"I gave Robert about an hour, maybe a little longer...to fall asleep. I guess it was about midnight," Long answered.

"And you rode straight to the Reeves' place, eight or ten miles away, in Grove? About what time, would you say, you got there?"

"Yes, sir...'er, not exactly. My horse was penned in the barn, and it took me near to an hour to round up Jim's horse, 'cause he had let it out in the pasture. And I didn't ride straight to old man Reeves' - I rode up near to Mark Peters' place and tied the horse in some bushes...eh...I done forgot the question now."

"Can you estimate what time it was when you reached Mark Peters' place?"

"It had to be close to 2 o'clock...if not a little later. It was so dark, I couldn't ride full out...I sure didn't want Jim's horse to stumble and break a leg or nothin'...so I loped her....it took me over an hour..."

From there, Johnie went on to describe the events of the evening. The defense attorneys, especially W. C. Barnette, objected frequently. They were usually over-ruled.

"Johnie, when you were first arrested, you made a confession—you confessed that you were coerced by Henry Waller into going to Mr. Reeves' to play cards and drink, were you not?"

"Objection! Your honor, the prosecutor is leading this witness," Barnette was red-faced and furious.

"Mr. Drew...." Judge Sandlin peered at Drew over the top of his glasses. The look said enough.

"I apologize, your honor," Drew said, looking anything but repentant. "May I rephrase my question?"

"Do it carefully."

"Johnie, why would you go to all the trouble to sneak out of your parents' house in the middle of the night, round up an

80

unpenned horse, and ride 10 miles on Christmas to play a game of cards?"

"'Cause Henry told me to."

"Objection!"

"Over-ruled."

"Henry told you to? Henry Waller—that man sitting right there," Drew pointed to the defendant, smoldering at the defense table between his two attorneys.

"That's right. Henry told me I needed to go on up to Pa's and stay. Said he was going to Sarepta...so as to set up alibis...."

"Objection, your honor, the witness..."

"Over-ruled—let the witness continue, Mr. Barnette." Judge Sandlin's curiosity was peeked. Up until now, every single defendant had declared that the reason they went to Reeves' that night was to play cards and drink whiskey. They had only hinted that the reason might have been robbery. Or worse.

"So, what you're saying is that Henry Waller planned for you to meet him at the Reeves place on Christmas morning for some other purpose than to play cards and have a few drinks, is that right?" Drew asked. "And the reason you had to establish alibis was to avoid suspicion, right?"

"Objection!"

"Over-ruled."

"Is that right?"

"Yes, sir. I guess so. 'Cause a couple days before Christmas, Henry told me he had everthin' worked out."

"But didn't you question Henry's motives when he told you to visit your Pa's so you wouldn't be suspected? Suspected of what?" Drew hammered away.

"I wasn't rightly sure...I guess I figured Henry was gonna rob the old man. He didn't like him, ya know. But I never figured he'd do what he done—I never figured Henry was that mean. And Henry said there was no chance of us gettin' in trouble, cause we could throw it off on the negras."

"Objection, your honor...the witness is out of line."

"Sustained...Mr. Long, please keep your personal opinions to yourself."

"Yes, sir, I'm sorry," Johnie apologized, looking embarrassed and ill at ease.

Drew wasn't finished.

"When you say Henry Waller didn't like Mr. Reeves, what do you mean?"

"Objection, the prosecutor is leading the witness again."

"Sir, I'm just trying to establish the nature of the relationship between the victim and the defendant...by using this witness."

"Continue, Mr. Drew."

"Thank you, your honor," he said, turning back to Johnie. "Now, do you recall an incident during which gunfire was exchanged between Mr. Waller and Mr. Reeves?"

"Well, sir, there was that time last spring when they was all playing cards over to old man Reeves. Henry accused the old man 'a cheatin' and come home and got his shotgun. When he come back, they got into a shootin' match. Henry told me old man Reeves shot at him nine or ten times...but he only shot once."

"Objection—this is hearsay—the witness obviously wasn't there," Barnette spewed.

Judge Sandlin agreed.

"Sustained—jury please disregard what the witness just said. Mr. Long, you must confine your testimony to first-hand knowledge—not what you were 'told' by the defendant, or anyone else."

"I'm sorry...I really am."

But the tale was told.

"It's all right, Johnie," Drew reassured his witness. "Were there any run-ins that the two men had that you were witness to?"

"Well, there was that time just before Christmas...me and Henry was goin' over to Mr. Martin's to collect a bill. I told Henry that old man Reeves come to me and told me to tell him that he'd better forget about that shootin' business, cause he knew something on him that would get him in trouble for sure."

"Did he know something on Henry?"

"Well, first Henry said he was a damned liar...uh, I'm sorry for that curse word, sir...but that was exactly what Henry said. Then, on the way back home, he said that old son-of-a-bitch just might know something on him. Said he might know about some scheme he'd cooked up to steal some cotton. Henry said he was gonna have to take care of him. Said the old man would get him into trouble if he didn't get him first."

"How did he say he was going to take care of Mr. Reeves?"

82

"Objection, your honor."

"Over-ruled."

"Go ahead, Johnie."

"He didn't say exactly right then. But he told me I was gonna go with him. I said I didn't want no part of it. But he said I had to go...and that he'd come up with some way to blame it on the negras....Later, he come up with the alibis."

Drew feigned an incredulous look.

"Then you must have suspected that Henry was bent on doing some harm to Mr. Reeves, right Johnie? If you needed an alibi...and someone to blame something on. And you of all people knew what Henry Waller was capable of...so why on earth would you go along with him?"

"Henry said there was no way for me to get into trouble. 'I'll tell where I was...and you'll tell where you was...and we'll throw it off on the negras'—that's what he said. I told him agin I didn't want to be in on it. He said 'Yes, damn you, you'll be there or I'll do the same thing to you I'm gonna do to that son-of-a-bitch.' I was scared not to go along, Mr. Drew...that's all I can tell ya."

"You were afraid for your life?"

"Objection!"

"Sustained."

"Sorry, your honor, I just have one more question. Johnie, do you think you are a fairly intelligent man?"

The question was unexpected. Drew and the courtroom waited for the answer.

"Well, I guess I have pretty good sense for an ordinary country boy."

Drew nodded, as if to concur with the youth's self analysis. He walked to the prosecution table.

"Your witness," he said, and sat down.

****

Barnette's cross-examination took the form of an attack on Long's credibility - an attempt to impeach him as a dependable witness by sublimating the idea of a conspiracy between the witness and the Prosecution into the minds of the jurors.

"Were you promised an early release if you testified at this trial?" Barnette asked.

Drew stiffened noticeably in his chair.

"Your Honor, if my worthy colleague wants to suggest that the office of the District Attorney in any way acted improperly, I would like to approach the Bench so that we can settle this matter out of the presence of the jury," he said, remaining seated.

However, before the judge could rule, Long blurted out an answer.

"No, sir. No promises been made to me. Mr. Drew there, and Mr. Price, they heard my statement a couple of weeks ago. And it's the same one I'm tellin' today. I ain't gonna change it. I wasn't restin' real good before I told it...cause I changed it so much. But since I told it straight, I'm restin' easier in my mind. And Mr. Drew there, he just told me to tell the truth, and to name the man who committed the murder."

Drew's face remained impassive. Foster could barely contain a smile.

Barnette quickly changed the subject.

"Have you ever been sick, Mr. Long?"

"Oh, I had the normal fevers like most folks."

"Have you ever thought you might be going crazy?"

"Objection," Drew and Foster chortled like a fine-tuned duet.

"I have a reason for my question, Judge."

"It had better be a good one."

"Mr. Long, didn't you suggest at one time to Sheriff Phillips that you might be going crazy?"

"Well, sir, I told the sheriff that I was hurtin' mighty bad 'cause of the mess I was in and that I felt real bad about bein' in on it. But I don't think I'm crazy or nothin'."

"I see."

Barnette walked over to the Defense table and picked up a sheaf of papers.

"You wrote two letters to your parents while you were in jail, didn't you?"

"Yes, sir, I did."

"Your honor, I'd like to enter these two letters into evidence..." Barnette waved the letters in the direction of the Prosecution, and paused. "If there is no objection."

"We have no objection, judge."

"Consider them entered."

Barnette continued to hold the letters, but made no indication that he would read them. He dangled them in front of Long.

"Is it true that in both these letters you denied having anything to do with the murders?"

"Yes, sir, but..."

"But now you are here in this courtroom telling us that you know all about the murders....the murders that you said you didn't know anything about..."

"I didn't want my folks, especially Eva, to think I would do something like that," Long explained.

"So now you admit it...My goodness, Mr. Long, how you love spinning a yarn. Is there any reason we should believe that you are not now fabricating a story? How do we know that you would not also conspire to frame your friend Henry Waller...Did you conspire to frame him, Johnie?"

"Objection."

"Let him answer, Mr. Drew," Judge Sandlin ruled.

"Is that why you have to claim that your *friend* frightened you so much that you would take part in a murder—because you and the men who have already been convicted of this crime framed him?"

"Objection!" this time Drew was on his feet.

"Mr. Barnette, you are out of line...jury disregard that last statement by the defense...it is purely speculative."

But Johnie Long was already agitated.

"But I was scared, I was..." he squeaked. "Henry told me he'd do the same thing to me that he was going to do to that son-of-a-bitch Reeves. He told me if he didn't get me...he'd have someone else do it."

Johnie Long looked pleadingly at Henry Waller.

"Didn't you say that, Henry? Didn't you?"

Henry Waller sat motionless...staring at the floor.

****

Eva Anderson fidgeted nervously with her hair. She was very fond of her brother...and deep down blamed Henry Waller for all of his present problems. She knew Johnie was going to prison...there wasn't much she could do for him now. She had tried to protect him...as only an older sister can. But Waller had simply been too strong a force to reckon with.

85

Preliminary questions revealed that she, her husband, and their two children lived on the Waller place along with Johnie. She more or less took care of the household duties and cared for Henry's four children, who had lost their mother to a fever a little over a year ago.

"Mrs. Anderson, in your opinion, did Henry Waller have a notable influence over your brother?" Drew asked.

"Your honor, this question calls for speculation."

"I'm going to allow it, counselor...You may answer the question, Mrs. Anderson."

Eva chewed on her nail and hesitated before answering.

"It sure looked as if he did," she finally replied. "It seemed that Johnie would always do anything Henry told him to do."

"Can you be more specific...tell us about any particular incidents...."

"Objection!"

"Mr. Drew, I'm going to sustain Mr. Barnette's objection at this point."

Drew nodded and continued. "Mrs. Anderson, you returned home from your brother's on Tuesday following Christmas, didn't you?"

"Yes, I did."

"Do you recall anything happening the next day, on Wednesday, that might have seemed a little out of the ordinary?"

"Well, Henry got home that evening - Tuesday evening - and asked where Johnie was. I told him I didn't know. The next day, he went over to Grove to pick up some more of his things. He got back after dark, and I had fixed him some supper. He seemed very nervous and wasn't real interested in eating. He started pacing and kinda mumbling to himself...that's when I heard him say something about expecting to be arrested. I didn't know what to think when he suddenly grabbed his hat off his head, threw it on the floor, and stomped his feet. He said 'I wish the whole damned world would sink this minute!!' It kinda scared me."

"Did Henry mention Johnie?"

Eva hesitated.

"Are you frightened, Mrs. Anderson."

"Well, no sir," she laughed nervously. "I do recall Henry mentioning on Wednesday that if Johnie had stayed home from

Mike Martin's wedding, there wouldn't have been anything about 'it'—but I didn't know what he was talking about at the time."

"What do you think he was talking about now?"

"Well, I suppose he meant that Johnie had talked too much about the killings at the wedding. I seem to recall that Henry mentioned more than once that Johnie was talking too much."

"What else do you recall?"

"Well, I know for a fact that both Henry and Whit, that's his brother, expected that Henry was going to be arrested."

Drew looked at the jury, gauging their reaction to Eva's last statement.

"Thank you, Mrs. Anderson," he said, satisfied.

****

Jim Long had been subpoenaed by the Defense, so it surprised a few people when the Prosecution called him to the stand.

Questioned by Drew about the night his younger brother spent at their Pa's house, Jim Long expressed doubts about the likelihood of anyone being able to "hem-up" his horse and ride him 10 miles to Grove in such a short time.

"I had nailed up Johnie's horse in my stable with eight-penny nails," he told the court.

"Why did you do that?" Drew asked.

"Well, 'cause a horse I'd been keepin' for a fella broke loose the other week. I didn't want that to happen agin."

Long told Drew that he had seen his brother and some neighbor boys early Christmas eve night enjoying music. He didn't see Johnie later that night, however, because his brother had stayed at their Pa's house, not his.

Cross-examined by Barnette, Long repeated his story of stabling his brother's horse and turning his own into the unfenced field. Again he stressed the improbability of anyone other than himself catching the horse and bridling it.

"On Christmas day, did you notice that your horse had been ridden?" Barnette asked.

"Not really. I needed my horse that afternoon, so two of my younger cousins caught him for me..."

Drew looked up...then at the jury, trying to determine whether or not they had caught the contradiction in Long's story. One minute the horse is in an open field with no fences, and impossible to catch, and the next it's being caught and saddled by two youngsters.

"You didn't see your brother late Sunday night because he slept over at your parents' home...when did you next see him?" The inconsistency hadn't escaped Barnette, and he was ready to move on.

"Guess I didn't see him again til Monday mornin' - yeah, Christmas morning."

"And how did your brother look to you on Christmas morning?" Barnette asked.

"He didn't look no different than usual."

"What about his clothing?"

"He had some mud on his trousers...but he told me he'd slipped in some mud. And I believed him, ya know...Johnie's kinda clumsy and all..."

"Did you and he talk?"

"We talked a little."

"Did he mention anything to you at all about the previous night's activities?"

"Not really...," Long hesitated. "Well, he did mention...I can't remember exactly when...that he might be havin' trouble in court."

Drew and Foster exchanged knowing looks and marveled at their luck.

The Defense, it seemed, was doing their job for them...

****

The Prosecution's next several witnesses were called for the express purpose of establishing a motive.

Brown Lipscomb was asked if, on Saturday, December 23, 1916, he had heard Waller make threats against Reeves at a Minden store. Sure, he heard Waller make threats, he said, but he couldn't recall anyone's name being mentioned.

Likewise, Ben Turner professed to hearing Waller make threats the prior spring. He, also, could not remember a specific name being called.

****

Sheriff Hutch Phillips was the last witness to testify Tuesday.

"Sheriff, did you have cause to examine the room where Johnie Long spent the night prior to Christmas day, 1916?" Drew asked.

"I did."

"At that time, did you notice anything peculiar about the planks around and above the bedroom door?"

"Objection, your honor," Barnette said, failing to qualify his complaint.

"I'm going to allow it, Counselor."

Phillips continued. "Yes, I noticed that they were very loose."

"They could have been removed easily?"

"Objection." Barnette again.

"Over-ruled."

"Yes, I would say they could have been removed easily enough."

Drew nodded his head and leaned over the prosecution table. He briefly conferred with Foster.

"Sheriff, on the Tuesday night after the murders, did you receive a phone call from Mr. Whit Waller who told you that he and his brother had just arrived home and that his brother Henry wanted to talk to you?"

"Your honor...I object!"

"Over-ruled...continue Sheriff Phillips!"

"Thank you, sir. Yes, Whit Waller phoned me up...then Henry took the phone."

"And what did he tell you?"

"He talked about how horrible the Reeves killing was...and offered to help me any way he could."

"Sheriff, did any other citizens of this parish made such an offer."

"Objection...what's the relevance of this question, your honor?"

"I'll allow it."

"During the course of the investigation, many citizens offered their assistance...," Sheriff Phillips answered. "But no one specifically called me up to make such an offer."

"That's all I have for this witness at this time." Drew nodded his thanks to the sheriff and sat down.

"Sheriff Phillips," Barnette chose to remain seated. "Do you remember seeing Henry Waller at the scene of the investigation Wednesday?"

"I believe he was there."

"And were there many other people there as well?"

"Yes."

"Did you notice anything unusual about Mr. Waller...did he act nervous or any way out of the ordinary?"

"I can't say that he did...I really didn't pay a whole lot of attention to Mr. Waller's appearance."

"Thank you. That's all."

Cody Reeves During the Trial
(Taken from the Webster Signal-Tribune)

Judge Harmon C. Drew
(Courtesy of Judge Harmon R. Drew, Jr.)

Luke M. Grigsby, chairman of the "Organization to Suppress All Lawlesness," is buried in the Shady Grove Cemetery, near the site of what once was the community known as Grove. Lelia Garrison Waller, the wife of Henry Waller, is buried nearby.

Front page from The Shreveport Times

The inscription of Judge John M. Sandlin's grave marker in the historic Minden Cemetery says, "To Know Him Was to Love Him." Buried next to him are his wife, Ruth, and his only daughter, baby Ruth. Reporter William Harper, who would later become editor and publisher of the Minden newspaper, is buried nearby.

Governor John M. Parker
(Photo Courtesy La. State Library)

Governor Ruffin G. Pleasant
(Photo Courtesy La. State Library)

Judgement...

State of Louisiana

vs.

Chester Tyson

State of Louisiana ◊
Parish of Webster ◊

No. *3/55*

Second Judicial District.

In this cause, by reason of the law and the evidence being in favor of the State and against the accused, and by further reason of the indictment and endorsements thereon, and considering the verdict of the Jury finding the accused guilty of MURDER as charged, *and after the accused, previous to sentence, asked what he had to say why the sentence* It is ordered, adjudged and decreed that the defendant, be hanged by the neck until he is dead

That *the officer designated by law* will execute this judgment according to law at a time and upon a day to be fixed by the Governor of the State of Louisiana.

Thus done, read and signed in open Court and in the presence of the accused on this the *30th* day of *January* 1917.

J. N. Sanders

Judge Second Judicial District.

"Considering the verdict of the jury finding the accused guilty of MURDER as charged, and after the accused, previous to sentence, was asked what he had to say why the sentence of the law should not be pronounced against him; it is ordered, adjudged, and decreed that the defendant, Chester Tyson, be hanged by the neck until he is dead."

"Sheriff Hughes, did you personally arrest Johnie Long after a warrant for his arrest was issued on the evening of December 28, 1916?"

The Caddo Parish sheriff was the first witness called by the State Wednesday morning and Harmon Drew was wasting no time getting down to business.

"That's right. At Sheriff Phillips' request, my chief deputy and I accompanied him over to Webster Parish to arrest Mr. Long and Mr. Henry Waller. Mr. Long rode back to Shreveport in my car, and Waller was accompanied by Sheriff Phillips and his men."

"And, without any coercion or force or your part, Mr. Long made a statement while you were driving from Germantown to Shreveport?"

"Yes."

"In that statement, did he accuse Henry M. Waller of murdering John Nelson Reeves and his family?"

"Yes, he did."

"And when you arrived at your jail, you had Mr. Long repeat what he told you in the motor car?"

"I had him repeat it. Then I wrote his statement out in longhand, and I had Mr. Long read it, and sign it."

"Thank you, Sheriff."

Judge Sandlin looked toward the defense table.

"Mr. Barnette....Mr. Robertson...any questions for this witness?"

"Yes, your honor, I have a few questions," Barnette said, rising. "Sheriff Hughes, after Johnie Long signed this alleged confession, what did you do?"

"I visited the cell where Mr. Waller was being held........."

Sheriff Hughes, thinking back, recounted the visit for Barnette and the jury.

He could easily remember the look of panic that had come into Henry Waller's eyes while he was telling him about Long's accusations. He had then handed the signed confession to Waller to read.

91

Suddenly, Waller threw the paper to the floor and covered his face with his hands. He backed away, moaning, until he was pressed against his bunk. Without warning, he started forward, grabbed the cell bars and began praying out loud, "Oh, Lord what will I do? What am I going to do?" His knees must have buckled then, because he dropped to the floor, still gripping the bars. He looked imploringly at Sheriff Hughes, genuine fear reflected in his eyes.

He remembered exactly what Henry Waller said next.

"Don't let no lynch mob get me Sheriff...you got to protect me, please don't let 'em get me."

"What did you tell him...after he begged you for protection?" Barnette asked, when the Sheriff paused.

"I told him that no lynch mob was going to harm him as long as he was in my custody."

"And what was his response?"

"He told me he could prove by fair trial where he was that night."

"No more questions, your honor."

Caddo Jailer Tillman Gambin corroborated Sheriff Hughes' testimony.

"Waller went up in the air more than any man I ever handled in jail," Gambin remarked at one point.

****

Grady Braselton leaned forward on the stand, his arms resting on the railing and his pudgy fingers fiddling with a loose thread on his sleeve. His eyes never left Harmon Drew's face.

"Sir, do you recall an incident that took place a week before the Reeves murders during which time Henry Waller told you about a lot of money?"

"Judge, I object to this line of questioning, since it is obviously going to involve hear-say evidence," Barnette said.

Drew persisted.

"Your Honor, this doesn't fall into the 'hear-say' category, since we have one witness testifying to what was said by the defendant in this case, not by a third party. The State feels that it certainly lays the groundwork for motive. We think this testimony is vital."

"I'm going to allow it," Judge Sandlin said.

"Mr. Braselton, do you recall such an incident?"

92

Braselton jumped at the mention of his name.

"Yes, sir," he answered. "It was on the Saturday 'afore the killin's. Henry come to me and said old man Reeves had shown him a big roll a money...said it was 'atween two thousant and four thousant dollars."

"Thank you....by the way, do you remember anything Mr. Waller said to you a day or two after the Reeves murders?"

"Well sir, on Wednesday Henry come over to Grove...I believe he was gettin' some more of his stuff moved...and he asked if the law didn't suspect nobody in that Reeves case or if'n anybody had been arrested."

****

Once more, Mark Peters found himself on the witness stand in the Webster Parish Courthouse, a place he thought he'd never see again—except in his dreams.

Once again he told how, during the early morning hours of December 25, 1916, Henry Waller, Johnie Long, and Chester Tyson came to his house and "enticed" him to accompany them to John Reeves' home for some fun and frolic and simple robbery.

Once again he denied any pre-knowledge of the crime.

This time, he admitted being in the house, standing at the foot of the bed, when Waller - yes, Henry Waller - struck the first blow that ripped open John Reeves' head. That was how he got blood on his shoes, he said. The blood splattered out onto them as the ax crushed into the old man's skull. He ran from the house....and puked his guts out.

Was Larkin Stewart there?

Yes, he was.

After the killings, he and Chester and Larkin left, returning home through a field. The last time he saw the two white men, they were walking toward the front gate...

Drew found himself questioning a much calmer man than he had convicted and sent to Death Row in January. Mark Peters had come to the realization that he was doomed. And now was the time to tell the truth. He seemed at ease, sat back in his chair in a relaxed manner, and looked Drew in the eye when he answered.

"Mark, has anyone visited you in prison at Angola?" Drew asked the question.

"Yes, sir."

"Do you remember their names?"

"A Mr. Sullivans...he come to visit with the prison preacher man."

"Did he ask you about the Reeves murder...?"

"Yes, sir. He done told me I could helps myself by tellin' that I didn't have nuthin' ta do with them killin's. So, I told that preacher man I didn't."

"But you weren't telling the truth, were you?"

"No..."

"Have you told us the truth here today?"

"Yes"

"Were you promised anything? Are you going to benefit by telling the truth here today?"

"Nobody promised me nuthin'. I know I ain't gonna escape that noose...nobody gonna help me now. I ain't lookin' for anything 'cept what they promised me right here in this courthouse - death."

Defense attorney Barnette, cross-examining the convicted killer, was incredulous.

"Mr. Peters, did you not tell Ed Sullivan, a former Marshall for this city...in the presence of Rev. Johns, the prison chaplain...while you were under sentence to hang at the state penitentiary...did you not tell Mr. Sullivan and Rev. Johns that you lied when you said you had knowledge of the crime...that you did not participate in the crime? Did you not repudiate your earlier confession...telling Mr. Sullivan, and I quote 'Well, boss, I don't want to die with a lie on my lips,' and that you were finally going to tell the truth?"

"I...uh..."

"Did you not tell the DeSoto Parish sheriff the same thing while you were incarcerated in jail in Mansfield prior to your trial...did you not deny having any knowledge of this crime?" Barnette raged on.

"I told Mr. Sullivan that. Yes, I prob'ly told that sheriff that."

"Do you always lie, Mr. Peters? How can this court believe what you say...how can this court believe anything you say...when you admit that you have lied on so many occasions..."

"'Cause I thought it might help me...might do me some good if I lied to that prison preacher and that Mr. Sullivan...He told me it would do me some good. I didn't know they was gonna bring me back to Minden. I figured it couldn't do nothin' but help me....'cause they was gonna hang me...what I got to lose by tellin' 'em I didn't have nothin' ta do with it?"

"So you admit that you are a liar?"

"Objection," Drew barked.

"Sustained, Mr. Barnette you might want to consider rephrasing your question."

"All right. Mr. Peters, you admit that you have failed to tell the truth time and time again. So why should we believe that you are telling us the truth today when you say that you know who killed Mr. Reeves. How do we know that you are telling us the truth at all—that you did not, in fact, kill John Reeves yourself?"

"Objection, your honor..."

But Mark Peters was already on his feet, glaring at the Defense attorney. "No, sir," he said, his words carrying steel. "I didn't kill nobody...Henry Waller killed them people...that man sittin' right there used that ax!!"

He pointed and glared at Henry Waller.

****

Yes, Chester Tyson told the court, he had also been visited by Mr. Sullivan and Chaplain Johns. Unlike Mark Peters, he had refused to change his story. He stuck to his original confession, the one he made to "undercover" detective Will Lloyd in the Texarkana jail.

The one that had earned him the death sentence.

Waller had come to his house after he had gone to bed Christmas eve night. He told him he didn't want to go because he was getting married the next day and needed his sleep. Waller persuaded him to go. As they were leaving, Waller picked up the ax—said they might need it to chop pine if they played "pitch" in the pasture.

When the two neared Mark Peters' house, Tyson could see Long, Stewart, and Peters waiting for them.

"You're telling us that Mark Peters was already outside the house...that Henry Waller didn't have to call him out...you're positive about that?" Drew looked mystified.

"That's right...I'm positive 'bout it," Chester replied, continuing.

When the quintet arrived at the Reeves, Waller, Long and Peters went into the house while he and Stewart remained outside.

He heard a lot of hollerin'. He saw Mrs. Reeves run out of the house, pursued by Henry. They disappeared around the side of the house. He never entered the house, and he didn't break open the storage chest, like Johnie Long said.

Henry gave him Reeves' gun and he carried it home.

How was Waller dressed?

He didn't remember.

How did Waller come and go?

He didn't notice.

Thank you.

Your honor, the Defense rests.

****

Hoping to avoid a public confrontation, Sheriff Hughes, Deputy Bazer, and several other armed deputies escorted Peters and Tyson from the Webster Parish Jail to the L&A Depot as soon as the State rested its case.

Unfortunately, scores of people milling outside the courthouse, disappointed at not being able to get in, followed the armed entourage to the station, hoping to get a glimpse of the convicted killers. To Hughes' surprise, the crowd conducted itself in a civil manner and no one attempted to board the train. Peters and Tyson arrived at the Central Station in Shreveport safely.

****

D. Whit Waller, brother of Henry Waller and a "sometime" preacher, was the first witness sworn by the defense Wednesday afternoon.

He took the stand shortly after 2 o'clock, following the 30-minute recess called by Judge Sandlin. Drew had thrown the court somewhat out of balance when he rested the State's case very soon after returning from the noon break.

A widower like his brother, Whit and his children shared the noon meal at Henry's place on Christmas eve before they all left for Sarepta. He lived very near Henry in Germantown.

Barnette did the questioning.

"Mr. Waller, how far is your home from the Reeves place in Grove?"

"Oh, I'd say it's about eight miles."

"And how far would you say it is between Henry's home and your brother's home in Sarepta?"

"I'd figure about 28 or 30 miles."

96

Drew, sitting with his arms crossed across his chest, looked at the jury. Did they buy that last statement?

Barnette continued. "And so you set out after lunch for Sarepta. How many of you were there and how did you travel?"

"Well, besides Henry and myself, there was Henry's four boys and my four - I got two daughters and two sons—guess that makes 10 of us altogether. We went by wagon...used one of my mules and a horse of Henry's."

"Tell us about the trip...was it eventful?"

"Not really...'bout a mile or two down the road we stopped at the widow Krouse's and talked to cousin Ben Wrenn and Parson Griffin for 10 or 15 minutes. Didn't do much more stoppin' after that. Coupla miles out 'a Sarepta, it was after dark, we asked a fella on horseback - I wasn't familiar with him - if he knew if our brother Jesse was to home or over to Judge Coyle's. He told us he thought he was still home."

"And what time did you arrive at your brother's?"

"I reckon it was about 7 -- we drove unreasonable fast though."

"What did you do then?"

"Took us about an hour to eat supper—then me and the kids went on over to my sister's, who is married to Walter Dean.

"Did Henry accompany you?"

"He come later with Jesse."

"What's the distance from Jesse's to your sister's?"

"Oh, not more 'n a quarter of a mile."

"Everybody was there?"

"Well, me an' the kids, Henry and his boys, Jesse and Jennie, sis and Walter, and their kids...oh, and Mr. William...that's Walter's father...he was there."

"How long did you stay?"

"Me and the kids stayed the night there."

"When did Henry and Jesse leave?"

"I'd say it was about 11 o'clock."

"And when did you see your brother Henry again?"

"The next morning—he come back over to Walter's."

"Was it early?"

"Bright and early."

On cross-examination, brother Whit proved a predictably hostile witness for the Prosecution.

97

"Did your brother Henry come to your house on Saturday, December 23 to ask you to accompany him to Sarepta the next day?" Drew asked.

"I really don't remember." Waller sat back in the chair and crossed his arms over his chest. He didn't bother to hide his animosity from the chief prosecutor.

"Where did you spend the night of December 23?"

"At home."

"The horse and mule...were they hitched up at your place or Henry's."

"At my place."

"And how did Henry's horse get there?"

"I don't remember."

"Did you drive the team over to Henry's the next day?"

"I don't recall who drove."

"Or did Henry come over to your place and drive the team back to his home?"

"I don't remember."

"Or did you and the children, in fact, walk over to Henry's?"

"I don't remember."

"You told the court earlier that the distance from Henry's place in Germantown to your brother Jesse's place in Sarepta was 28 to 30 miles. Are you sure of that?"

"Well, that's hard to say...might be 30 -- might be 15...I've never measured it."

Drew was growing agitated.

"Excuse me for interrupting, Judge, but this witness is not an expert in distance and there's obviously a lot of difference between 15 miles and 30 miles. I object to his testimony being allowed."

"I might agree with you, counselor, but, without actually going out and measuring it, the only way we can ascertain the distance is by the opinion and knowledge of those who travel it. I'll have to rule that Mr. Waller falls into that category. I'll have to over-rule your objection and allow the testimony."

Drew's face registered dissatisfaction with the ruling.

"Mr. Waller, only one of your brother's horses, one that had never been ridden, was used on the trip from Germantown to Sarepta, is that not correct? Doesn't he have another horse?"

98

"Ms. Evie was using the other horse...she rode it up to Ward I to visit her family."

"And how far was that?"

"I'd guess it was about 12 miles."

"What I'd really like to know is how that mule of yours fared...after such a loooonng trip," Drew spit the rhetorical question at Waller.

Barnette was indignant.

"Judge I strongly object to the State's mocking tone with this witness."

"Sustained, watch yourself, Mr. Drew."

"I apologize, your honor," Drew said, tipping his head and locking eyes with Barnette. "But it would seem to me that this witness is not attempting in any way to cooperate with the State. We simply want straight answers."

He turned back to Whit Waller.

"For instance, Mr. Waller, did you not originally tell Jim Johnson that you passed no one on your way to Sarepta? And then later you told him you had?"

"I guess so," Waller's reply was reluctant. "I'd probably forgot."

"Did you know the rider that you met on the road to Sarepta? The one you asked about Jesse's whereabouts?" he asked.

"No."

"Was Henry acquainted with him?"

"I don't know."

"All right, Mr. Waller, let's return to Christmas morning and Henry arriving at the Dean's home...what time would you say he arrived there?"

"I didn't pay no attention to the time."

"Mr. Waller do you have a bad memory?"

"Objection, Mr. Drew is badgering the witness."

"I guess I do," Waller said, before Judge Sandlin could muster a reprimand.

"I guess you do," Drew said, and sat down.

****

The parade of witnesses called by the Defense to support Waller's alibi—his Christmas eve trip to visit relatives in Sarepta—seemed endless.

Ben F. Wrenn said he saw Whit and Henry and their children at about 2 o'clock Christmas eve at the widow Krouse's.

"Tell me, Mr. Wrenn, are you related to the Wallers?"

"You might say...we're kinda distant kin...I got a second cousin who married a Waller...but..."

"What a surprise," Drew's sarcasm was apparent. "Tell me something else, Mr. Wrenn, didn't you serve on the last Grand Jury?"

"Objection....that's irrelevant."

"Sustained."

Walter Roby testified that he passed a wagon while out riding in his car near Cotton Valley at about 5 p.m. Christmas eve...it was headed in the direction of Sarepta...but he didn't pay any attention to who was in it.

No, it wasn't uncommon to pass wagons.

W. T. Page, who resided three miles south of Cotton Valley, said he saw Henry Waller, another man, and a bunch of kids in a wagon pass by his house Christmas eve. No, he wasn't related to the Wallers. He had only met Henry Waller a few weeks before the killings. Someone had introduced them in Minden. No, he couldn't recall seeing any other wagons pass his way Christmas eve.

John E. Coyle, Jr. had been a rural mail carrier for seven years. He was the son of Justice of the Peace Coyle. His sister, Jennie, was married to Jesse Waller. He resided about three-quarters of a mile from Sarepta. At approximately 7:30 Christmas eve night, Henry Waller passed his house in a wagon and "hollered" at him. He didn't see him, but he heard Waller yell, "Hello, Johnny, Christmas eve gift!" No, it wasn't unusual for friends of his to "holler" at him even after he'd gone to bed.

Up near the Coyle home on Christmas eve night, between 7:20 and 7:30, Will Manry met some people he didn't know. He heard one man say to the other, "Ask him, maybe he'll know." The man then inquired as to whether or not Jesse Waller was still visiting at the Coyle's. He said he wasn't sure, but he thought they were home. The men then introduced themselves. Did he recall the color of the team of horses (or mules) pulling the wagon? No. How did he establish the time so specifically? He had just left the Sarepta Depot...and had looked at the clock as he was leaving.

Parson B. L. Griffith recalled having seen Henry and Whit Waller in a wagon on the road to Sarepta Christmas eve. Walter Dean's nephew, W.E. Wiley, said he didn't believe Jesse Waller's horse could make over five miles an hour. Frank Stanton said it would have taken a very long time for a wagon to get to Sarepta from the Reeves via the Cotton Valley Road. W.D. Bossier, who accompanied Stanton, didn't believe a round-trip between the two points could be made in a day's time.

Keefer Wiley said he saw Jesse and Henry Waller at a store in Sarepta at about 8 o'clock Christmas morning. Yes, he admitted, his sister married a Coyle, who was related to the Wallers by marriage.

S. L. Bibby said, yes, Jesse Waller owned a gray horse.

****

Jesse Waller was next on the stand. His memory was only slightly better than his brother's.

The wagon bearing Henry and Whit and their children had arrived at his home in Sarepta between 7 and 8 o'clock Christmas eve night. Whit's mule and Henry's horse were hitched to the wagon. Soon after their arrival, Whit and his children went over to Walter Dean's because Whit hadn't seen his sister in quite a while.

Later, he and Henry and their families also went to the Dean's. He couldn't be sure, because he hadn't looked at a clock, but it must have been around 11 or 12 midnight when they returned home. They put the children to bed, helped the wife prepare Santa Claus, and then stayed up talking for a while. They probably retired around 12:30 or 1 o'clock—although he didn't look at his timepiece, so he wasn't sure. Henry occupied a room next to Jesse's, sleeping with one of the youngsters.

The next time he saw Henry was Christmas morning. It was pretty early, because the kids waked them all up...excited about Santa Claus. They had breakfast, then went over to the Dean's—it was about sun-up. Yes, Henry went with them.

He and Henry left the Dean's, returned home to hitch up a horse, and rode to town for a shave.

Did you feed your stock Christmas morning?

Yes.

What about Henry's horse and Whit's mule?

Yes.

Notice anything unusual about any of the horses?

101

Nope, nothing unusual at all.

Harmon Drew cross-examined Jesse.

"Did you drink Christmas eve night?"

"Yeah, I had a few drinks."

"What about Henry."

"He mighta had one."

"Were you drunk?"

"No."

"Did you and Henry ride to the Evergreen Schoolhouse to attend a Christmas Tree Celebration on Christmas night?"

"Yes."

"What time did you leave home going to Evergreen?"

"About 5 o'clock."

"And about how far is it from Sarepta to Evergreen?"

"I don't know...'bout 18 or 20 miles."

"Mr. Waller, when was the first time that you heard about the murder of the Reeves family?"

"Objection."

"Over-ruled."

"At Evergreen."

"Was the killing freely discussed at the Christmas Tree?"

"Objection!"

"No," Waller replied, before the judge could respond.

"Mr. Waller, you say you and Henry helped your wife preparing Santa Claus for your children Christmas eve night...."

"That's right."

"Did you know that Mrs. Reeves was preparing Santa Claus for her own children the night they were brutally murdered......"

Barnette was on his feet.

"Objection...Objection, your honor."

"Sustained....Mr. Drew....that remark was uncalled for...I must ask you to watch yourself."

But Drew looked anything but contrite.

"I'd like to approach," Barnette said.

Judge Sandlin gestured for both men to come forward.

"Your honor...this reprehensible conduct on the part of the State must stop. I'd like to reserve a bill...objecting to the State's improper conduct and allowing that this statement prejudiced the jury and unduly gives them the wrong impression of my client."

"So taken into consideration, Mr. Barnette. Mr. Drew, maybe you need to let your assistant complete the questioning of this witness..."

It was not a suggestion.

"Yes, sir," Drew acquiesced, walking back to the Prosecution table. He sat down and whispered something to Foster, who bowed his head to hide a satisfied smirk before rearranging his papers and rising to his feet.

****

Jesse Waller had been sitting quietly on the witness stand during the bench confrontation. Like his brother, Whit, he made no attempt to mask his contempt for the Prosecutors. He looked at Foster as if to challenge him.

Foster was not intimidated.

"Mr. Waller, do you remember being instructed by Judge Sandlin not to discuss this case with anyone other than the lawyers?"

"Yes."

"Haven't you been talking to different witnesses—both State and Defense?"

"Objection."

"Over-ruled...I want to hear this," Judge Sandlin said.

"Yes." Waller's tone was defiant.

"Even though the court ordered you not to?"

"Yes, I guess."

"Haven't you, in fact, talked to some 10 or 12 witnesses...and sometimes more than once?"

"I don't know how many."

"Did you talk to them regarding their testimony?"

"I object, your honor...to this line of questioning."

"And I over-rule. Continue, Mr. Foster."

"Please answer my question, Mr. Waller...what did you talk to them about?"

"I don't rightly remember what I talked to them about. I probably wanted to know about what evidence the prosecutors might have...I think that's what I talked to them about...I got a right to know what evidence they got against my brother."

"Even if the court orders you not to talk to witnesses?" Foster's feigned look of astonishment was calculated to drive home a point.

"That's right," Waller replied, unaware of being mocked.

"No more questions, your honor."

"Redirect, Mr. Barnette?"

"No, sir, we're through with this witness."

****

More alibi witnesses.

Robertson asked the questions.

Miss Mamie Wiltheis told the court that Henry and Whit and their wagonload of children passed her house sometime between 2 and 4 in the afternoon. A mule and a gray horse were pulling the wagon. Yes, her brother, Porter Wiltheis, has been keeping Henry's horses since the arrest. No, she has never seen anybody ride Henry's horse...the one used on the trip to Sarepta.

How far do you live from the Reeves home?

About three miles.

Porter backed up his sister's testimony. He was keeping Henry's two horses. Yes, he was familiar with the gray horse. It appeared to be about six years old.

"Has the horse ever been ridden?" Robertson asked.

"Not so far as I know - I'd say it was pretty green."

"Do you think, Mr. Wiltheis, that this particular horse, Mr. Waller's horse, is capable of carrying a man 61 miles in three hours time?"

"We object, your honor, this man has not been identified as an expert witness," Drew offered.

"I'm going to over-rule your objection...let's hear what he has to say."

"Well, Mr. Wiltheis?" Robertson was impatient for the jury to hear the answer.

"I sure don't think so."

"Your witness, Mr. Drew," Robertson said, swaggering back to his seat.

Drew was undaunted.

"Mr. Wiltheis, why are you keeping Mr. Waller's horses?"

"I got a chattel mortgage on 'em."

"So you're telling us that you loaned Mr. Waller the money to purchase a crippled horse...a horse that can't be ridden...couldn't carry a man of Mr. Waller's slight build 60 miles...might as well shoot that horse, wouldn't you say, Mr. Wiltheis?"

104

"Objection, this is preposterous," Robertson was raging. "Judge, Mr. Drew is out-of-bounds...and he has no qualified right to ask such a question. We reserve a bill objecting to this line of questioning."

"So recorded. Mr. Drew, watch yourself."

"Yes, sir," he replied, turning his attention back to the witness. "Just what is the mortgage on this prize-winning horse?" Drew drawled, needling Robertson.

"Up front, a hunerd an' fifty...With intrest...one sixty one."

"My, my...quite a lot of money for such a poor, pitiful animal..."

"Objection...objection...Judge, please...."

"Would you like to reserve another bill?" Judge Sandlin headed Robertson off.

"Of course, your honor."

"So recorded...Mr. Drew have you got any more allowable questions for this witness?"

"Yes, sir. The State would like to know whether or not Mr. Waller has corresponded with Mr. Wiltheis regarding his livestock since his incarceration?"

"Objection, your honor, there has been no precedence set for this question."

"Sustained."

****

Wm. H. Dean was Walter Dean's father. He testified about the Waller and Dean families visiting Christmas Eve night at his son's home near Sarepta. Henry and Jesse left at 11 or 11:30, and the next time he saw them was 7:30 or 8 o'clock Christmas morning in town. Henry wanted a shave, he said.

He guessed it was about 20 miles from his son's home to the Reeves' place.

Dwight Waller, the 12-year-old son of Whit, corroborated his father's story about the trip from Germantown to Sarepta.

Thomas Waller, 10-year-old son of Henry, also testified.

"Thomas, do you remember your father and uncle coming in from visiting the Deans on Christmas Eve night—were you still awake?"

"Yes, sir. I mean, I'd already gone to bed...but I could hear 'em. And I heard 'em gettin' ready for Santa Claus and all."

105

"Do you remember seeing your father early the next morning?"

"I knowed he got up early...but I didn't see 'im on account of Aunt Jennie not lettin' us get up real early."

One by one, the defendant's relatives testified. Walter Dean, Jesse Dean, and Jennie Waller all told virtually the same story about Henry's movements Christmas eve night and Christmas morning.

"Your honor, the Defense would like to request about 10 minutes to get our next witnesses in order."

****

His request for a 10-minute recess granted, Barnette sat down and began talking seriously with Robertson and Judge Coyle.

Henry Waller turned and motioned at three little boys who were occupying a front row with their many relatives and friends. The littlest of the three, who was barefooted, climbed onto his lap. Holding the four-year-old to him, he leaned down and hugged all three simultaneously.

Judge Sandlin made no attempt to discourage the rare family reunion. It might be a long time before these children got to hug their father again. Henry's sister, who occupied a seat on the front row watching over her brother's children, sobbed loudly.

****

Barnette apparently changed his mind about calling another procession of witnesses.

"The Defense has many more witnesses to call, your honor, but we have only one other witness we'd like to bring to the stand at this time."

Judge Sandlin took out his timepiece, ignoring the oversized clock on the wall. It read 6:48 p.m.

"Because of the lateness of the hour, I'm going to allow you to call this one last witness. We'll resume testimony at 9 o'clock sharp in the morning. Go ahead and call your witness, Mr. Barnette."

The witness, Cotton Valley timberman W. T. Gleason, had a reputation for being somewhat of an expert on horses. He had been asked by Robertson and Barnette to measure the distance between Jesse Waller's house near Sarepta and the Reeves home in the Grove community.

106

"Mr. Gleason, you measured the distance from Jesse Waller's place to the Reeves' place at the request of this court, did you not?"

"Yes, I did."

"What did you come up with?"

"I measured the distance at precisely 19 miles."

"Mr. Gleason, you being an expert on horses, how fast would you say the average horse can travel?"

"Well, an average horse...that's a horse in fairly good condition...can travel about six miles per hour. That's on a 40-mile round trip...Anything longer than that and the horse would begin to tire and slow down."

"So, if the distance from Jesse Waller's to the Reeves place and back were 38 miles...an average horse would take over six hours to make the trip," Barnette directed his comments more toward the jury than Gleason.

"That's what my arithmetic tells me," Gleason smiled.

"No more questions, your honor." He gestured towards Drew, who stood and walked towards the witness.

"Mr. Gleason, you're a timberman...how did you come to gain such a reputation with horses?"

"I buy and sell 'em...Have for several years...sometimes there's more profit in it than timber."

"You say the average horse can travel six miles an hour...upon what do you base this conclusion?"

"Running the horses...testing them...racing them."

"Horses can't be forced to run faster...even an average horse?"

"Oh, sure, I've seen plenty of horses travel as fast as 12 miles an hour...Six is just an average, you see. 'Specially if the trip is anything less than 40 miles...They can pretty much keep up their stamina to that point."

Barnette flinched.

Drew, mimicking the defense attorney, directed his next comments to the jury.

"So, let's say a horse travels 38 miles at 10 miles per hour—uh, that's less than four hours, is it not?"

He turned back to the witness.

"You're as good a mathematician as that Mr. Barnette," Gleason said, smiling.

It was barely daylight, but folks were already lined up in front of the columnar entrance to the stately Webster Parish Courthouse. Since seating was limited and standing in the aisles had been prohibited by Judge Sandlin, being close to those massive double doors of justice meant everything.

Seasoned court observers could sense that the end of the trial was near...and the accused had yet to testify.

Would he testify? That was the hottest topic of conversation for the crowd.

Talk flowed as fast as the thick, black steaming coffee.

Was Waller bein' framed? Would he be convicted, and, if so, would he be sentenced to hang like Tyson and Peters? Had they set an execution date for those fellas yet? Aw, justice was just way too slow...Well, they did have to keep 'em alive to testify you know...

Special deputies appeared at the doors.

The crowd surged forward...

Day four was about to begin.

****

Rev. J.H. Alford of Colfax, a former pastor for a Sarepta church, took the stand first as the defense resumed its efforts to prove that Henry Waller could not have ridden a horse to Grove, butchered five people, and then raced the horse back to Sarepta in the time allotted to him.

The reverend said that he and Sarepta merchant, W.E. Allen, measured the distance from Sarepta to Knuckles Ford on Bayou Dorcheat with an automobile speedometer and by stepping a short ways to the actual crossing. Knuckles Ford was one of the most common crossings on the bayou and the one alleged to have been used by the defendant. Rev. Alford said that he and Mr. Allen determined the distance to be about 13.5 miles.

Felix Temple, a sewing machine agent, was the one commissioned by attorney Robertson to measure the distance from Knuckles Ford to the Reeves home. He confirmed that the distance measured 6.5 miles.

Barnette pointed out that, lest anyone fall short in the arithmetic department, that was 20 miles.

Harmon Drew, apparently as astute in arithmetic as his esteemed opponent, asked no questions of either Alford or Temple.

"Judge, before we call any more witnesses, we'd like permission to use several letters written by Johnie Long while he was incarcerated in Caddo Parish. We don't plan to read them at this time, we just want to take care of this matter." T.W. Robertson gestured towards the judge with the letters that had been entered into evidence earlier.

"Do you have any objections to the defense reading these letters later?" Judge Sandlin directed his question to Drew and Foster.

"Not at all," Drew responded, mildly surprised.

"Consider them entered."

Robertson thanked the judged.

Barnette called his next witness.

Rev. H. S. Johns was the chaplain for the Louisiana State Penitentiary at Angola. His testimony marked the beginning of a new defense strategy—that of discrediting the State's witnesses.

"Brother Johns, just last week you accompanied a visitor when he met with Chester Tyson and Mark Peters in their individual cells at the state prison, did you not?"

"That's correct, sir. Mr. Ed E. Sullivan asked Superintendent Fuqua if he could be allowed to visit with the men. Mr. Fuqua asked if I minded accompanying him, and I agreed."

"And Mr. Sullivan asked each man about the Reeves family being murdered, did he not?"

"He did."

"Did Mr. Sullivan try in any way to induce Mr. Tyson or Mr. Peters to admit to the killings? Did he promise them anything or assure them of anything?"

"No, fact of the matter is, he told each man that he could do nothing for them. He just wanted to hear the truth."

"And did they tell the truth?"

"Well, they both repudiated their earlier confessions."

"Your honor, the State objects to this line of questioning," Drew spoke for the first time. "It's an obvious smoke-screen and a waste of this court's time. Mark Peters and Chester Tyson have already testified at this trial. And both men readily admitted changing their stories. And they told why they changed their stories. This is pure grand-standing."

"I'll have to agree with Mr. Drew," Judge Sandlin replied. "Objection sustained. Do you have any more questions for this witness, Mr. Barnette?"

"No sir, but we would like to call Mr. Sullivan to the stand, if the court will allow..."

Mr. Ed E. Sullivan was secretary of the Minden Benevolent Society. He was a former Minden town marshall, a former justice of the peace, and a former school board member. He was on business in Baton Rouge when he decided to visit the incarcerated Tyson and Peters.

"Did you tell Chester Tyson or Mark Peters that changing their testimony could save their necks?" Barnette was being careful not to directly ask whether or not the two men altered their confessions.

"No, I did not."

"Did you encourage the men to change their statements?"

"No I did not."

"And Bro. Johns was with you at all times?"

"Every moment."

"Thank you, Mr. Sullivan."

Drew stood, but made no move toward the witness, preferring instead to remain locked between his chair and the table. He stared at Sullivan a few seconds before asking his first question.

"Mr. Sullivan, you've not been living in this area all that long have you?"

"On the contrary, I'm a native of this area. I moved back here last July after spending about five years in Texas and Shreveport."

"So, after living back in Minden for less than a year, you just up and decide to have a talk with two convicted murderers at the State Penitentiary?"

"Objection, your honor, I don't see the relevance to this line of questioning."

"Sustained."

"Then let me ask you this, Mr. Sullivan...who paid for your trip to the State penitentiary?"

"I was on business in Baton Rouge...with the Secretary of State...I paid my own expenses."

110

"Let me remind you that you are under oath when I ask you this next question, sir. Did you not tell Mark Peters and Chester Tyson that they could benefit from changing their stories?"

"I object!" Barnette looked frenzied.

Judge Sandlin raised an eyebrow at Drew.

"Your honor, it's the defense that insists on telling and retelling this story. I'm just wanting some straight answers."

"I agree. Objection over-ruled. Sit down, Mr. Barnette."

Drew looked decidedly smug.

"Thank-you, your honor. Now, Mr. Sullivan, are you sure that you in no way misled one or both of these men into thinking that they could benefit from changing their testimony?"

"All I told them was that it might help them...What I meant was it might help them to feel better. They mighta misunderstood...but I just meant it might help them feel better."

"Oh, I'm sure it did, Mr. Sullivan. Eh, I have just one more question. When these men told you what they told you...who did you tell?"

"I told Mr. Robertson."

"You told Mr. Robertson?" Drew pointed to the co-defense counselor. "No one else? You didn't tell the sheriff...you didn't tell the District Attorney...you just told Mr. Robertson?"

"Yes, I told Mr. Robertson—he's the one who asked me to make the visit."

Drew looked toward the jury and cocked an eyebrow.

"We have no more questions for this witness, your honor."

Barnette sprang immediately to his feet, apparently willing to concede the skirmish to Drew, but undaunted in his resolve to win the war. "No redirect, your honor. We'd now like to call Mr. Benjamin Wrenn."

As a court employee, Wrenn had more access to certain areas of the building, including the sequestering room. He had talked to Chester Tyson on Wednesday after the convicted murderer had left the stand.

"During his testimony in this court yesterday, Chester Tyson once again changed his story," Barnette stood close to Wrenn. Seated, Harmon Drew folded his arms over his chest, stretched his legs, and heaved a sigh. He couldn't believe Barnette was beating this dead horse again. But the defense attorney continued.

"Chester said he had lied to save his neck, then told the truth, then lied to save his neck again...and yesterday he once again owned up to his part in the killings. Do you remember that?"

"Yes, I do."

"But you talked to Mr. Tyson after he left the stand, didn't you?"

"Yes, I did."

"And what did he tell you."

"He told me he wasn't near the Reeves place on Christmas eve night...that he slept over with Anderson Heard."

"That was just yesterday...just after he testified in this court that he took part in the killings?"

"That's right."

"So, when he talked to you, did he say he knew anything about the killings...about who was responsible."

"No, he did not."

"No further questions, your honor."

Drew, still seated, shook his head when Judge Sandlin looked to him for cross-examination.

"Believe me, sir, we have no questions."

****

"Your honor, I'd now like to read this letter aloud to the jury," Robertson sauntered towards the jury waving several pieces of paper in his hand.

Testimony had resumed immediately after a short lunch break.

"Proceed, Mr. Robertson."

"This is a letter dated January 10, 1917 and addressed to Mr. and Mrs. J.P. Long and family."

He began to read.

"I will write you all a few lines to let you know how I am getting along. I am not doing well at all. I am just sitting here grieving my life away. This is the most mournful hours I ever spent in all my life. Now if I had of been in that murderin' scrape I wouldn't be grieving so bad. Just to think this poor boy has to suffer for what somebody else done, it is a shame. I don't know no more about that than you do. I couldn't tell you no more about how that was done than any other man that wasn't in it."

Robertson read the letter haltingly, sometimes pausing to make out Johnie Long's writing.

"Pa, I'd just as well be dead as alive. I don't believe I have got a friend in the world. Somebody told that they saw me about twelve miles from up there that Sunday night about 12 o'clock in the night and you know that is a lie, don't you? And somebody told that they seen me trying to hire a car that night and the good lord in heaven knows that ain't so for I diden have the money to hire a car with. The man that told that lie he ain't got backbone a nuff to stand in my face and tell me that. For you know I stayed there Sunday night and if I am not mistaken I left my shoes in you all's room. I am not sure, but I think I did. Those Negroes told that Henry and myself made them do that."

Robertson paused again, when he resumed reading, his voice was louder.

"I don't know what Henry done, but I do know that I did'n. If I was to be hung this morning I would swear that I diden do that. What in the world would I of wanted to of told them Negroes to do that for? I diden have nothing aginst the old man and I diden know that he had any money and what in the world would I of wanted them to of done that for? I have found out now that it won't do to have any thing to do with a Negro for if they ever get in any truble themselves they will bring you in just as sure as your living they will do it. I am going to be sent to the pen on the count of it. Just as sure as the world stands and that will be awful to have to go on the count of a stankin god dam black Negro. If I ever get out of the pen I am going to when a Negro asks me for anything I am going to hall away and knock the hell right out of him just as soon as he asks me."

Resuming his normal voice, Robertson read on.

"Well, Pa, I guess you all will get tired of reading this scratches so I will rang off for this time. Tell Jim and Marry and all of them howdy for me, and Pa, you all come to my trial when it comes off for it may be the last time I will ever get to see any of you all. I don't know. You and Jim and the boys come if the rest can't come. You all come, Pa. You can go down there and get my trunk and all my clothes and keep them and all of them you can wear, you can have them. And them you can't, you let the boys have them. I guess you have got Eva with you, ain't you? And if you ain't, you get her and tell her that I said not to grieve after me for I don't know wether I'll see her anymore unless I see her at the courthouse. Tell her if she don't want to come see me that I can't

113

help it. May God bless her the longest day she lives. Tell her that I always thought she was more dear to me that either one of my other sisters and she done more for me than any of the others. Tell her now if she don't want to see me any more I can't help it. May God bless her. Will you go down there and get them things what I was talking about and the trunk is locked but I will give you the key at the courthouse. I have a nice new pair of pants in my trunk if you or any of the boys can wear them, Pa. I have a blue serge coat down there and I have a blue suit and if you can wear that coat or that blue suit you can have them and if you can't wear the blue suit, give it to Jim. I know you can wear that other blue coat. Now you be sure and get them and you all can have them for I won't need them when I get out younder. I will put on a different suit."

Robertson was squinting at the paper.

"Pa, I guess you all had done found out where I was, hadn't you. I am in Shreveport and Henry is in Baton Rouge. They said they had a feelin for me as a boy but they didn't have none for Henry and they sent him off the next day after we got here. Well Pa, I will close for this time as I am grieving so that I can hardly write. So give my love to all and kiss the children for me. So goodbye to all and God bless you to live happy the rest of your days. Pa, I sure did 'preciate that dollar you sent me for I didn't have a cent to my name. I sure was pride to get it. Thank you very much, Pa.. You all better not answer this letter. They don't want nobody to know where I am at. Yours Truly, Johnie Long."

As Robertson read Johnie Long's name he walked slowly in front of the jurors, tilting the letter so that each juror could get a view of the signature.

****

Sticking to their strategy of discrediting Long and therefore impeaching the State's star witness, the defense next called several young men who testified about sleeping over at the Long's house Christmas eve night.

A cousin, Lawrence Allen, confirmed that he had slept in the same room with Johnie. He did not hear him leave at any time during the night. Earlier that night, he (Johnie) had soiled his trousers when he slipped in some mud returning from a wedding.

Long's stepbrother, 14-year-old Robert Mobley, testified that he slept in the same room with Johnie and Lawrence, and that he (Johnie) had taken off some of his clothes in his mother's

114

room—probably because they were soiled. He said he awakened several times during the night because of a headache.

"And was Johnie there each time you awakened?"

"Yes, sir."

"What time did you see Johnie on Christmas morning?" Robertson asked.

"He wasn't up yet when I got up," Mobley said.

Robertson next called Johnie's father, J. P. Long.

"Your son spent the night at your home Christmas eve night, didn't he?" Robertson asked.

"Yes, he did."

"Do you remember what time he went to bed?"

"Well, let's see. He undressed in our bedroom...then went across the hall to join the other boys....it was probably 11:30."

"And you saw him early the next morning?"

"Yes...just after daylight."

"Is it true that the door to the room the boys were sleeping in was secured from the outside?"

"Yes, I had latched the door on the outside when the boys went to bed...Generally I wake 'em up the next day by unlatchin' the door. 'Course, like most boys, they was hard to wake up. Took a little proddin'...It was probably well after daylight that they began stirrin'."

"But Johnie was in the room when you unlatched the door and awakened the boys?"

"Yes, he was."

"Mr. Long, did Robert mention to you that he'd had a headache during the night?"

"Yes, he sure did mention it."

"I have no more questions of this witness, your honor."

"Mr. Drew...Mr. Foster?" Judge Sandlin looked toward the prosecutors.

"I just have two questions for Mr. Long at this time." Drew stood, but didn't approach the witness stand.

"Do you remember what your son was wearing when you saw him Christmas morning?" he asked.

"Well, he looked like he was wearin' what he always does...trousers...a work shirt..."

"Did you notice whether or not his clothes were soiled?"

"Yes, they was a little muddy."

115

"Do you remember, Mr. Long, what time the sun came up Christmas morning? Was it cloudy or sunny?"

"I can't say what time the sun come up...but I do remember it was cloudy...so it mighta appeared to come up later."

"No further questions."

Johnie Long's stepmother next testified that she sent the boys to bed around 11:30, and that before she awakened the next morning, Johnie was in her room "fetching" some articles of clothing he had left there the night before.

She noticed nothing unusual about his condition at that time.

****

William C. Barnette leaned toward his client at the defense table, taking advantage of a recess called by Judge Sandlin. Behind them, the admixture of voices ebbed and flowed from a crowd bent on "catching up" in the judge's absence.

To the client's right sat Barnette's partner, attorney Thomas W. Robertson, doodling on a pad. The table was also occupied by Webster Parish Deputy Sheriff Walter Dean, Justice of the Peace J.H.C. Coyle, and Dr. L. T. Waller.

The oft-ignored clock on the wall showed 2:05 p.m.

Barnette's voice was subdued to the point that his client was forced to turn his face sideways, converting his car into a virtual mouthpiece as he leaned and cocked his head.

"Do not...do you hear me...do not attempt to explain, rationalize, or justify anything when I ask you a question, you got that?"

The accused man nodded in understanding.

"When I ask you a question, simply give me an answer. If I ask you your name...tell me your name...if I ask you for an address, give me an address...when I ask you if you are guilty of murder...just say 'No'—don't try to offer any explanations—you got that?"

"Look, I'm not stupid...you've explained it to me a thousand times," the client's voice climbed a decibel above a whisper. A rigid scar just above his right temple throbbed.

The low drone of voices in the courtroom came to an abrupt halt.

Robertson motioned with his hand for the two to lower their voices.

116

"And I'm going to explain it to you one more time," Barnette said, acknowledging Robertson's warning with his eyes and a nod. "If you broach any subject area, then the Prosecution can ask you questions about it...Don't introduce anything to this court that you don't want to be questioned about later. This is very important?"

He feigned striking the desk with his fist and locked eyes with his client, daring him to say anything else.

****

"All rise."

Judge Sandlin walked back into the courtroom, seated himself at the bench, and looked wordlessly towards the Defense table.

In response, Barnette shoved back his chair, and stood up.

"Your Honor, the Defense would like to call Henry M. Waller to the stand."

At 5',7" tall and 145 pounds, Waller did not pose a striking figure. Nor did he appear malicious, evil, contemplative, vicious, threatening - any of those adjectives reserved for a cold-blooded killer. What he did look like with his ruddy skin and sallow, crowlike eyes was a heavy drinker. At 34, his black hair was just starting to whiten around the temples.

Barnette got the preliminary questions out of the way.

Waller was born in Alabama, raised in nearby Claiborne Parish, but had lived in Webster Parish for the past 17 years. He had moved to Germantown in early December from his farm in nearby Grove.

He had four children—all boys. He was a widower, his wife, Lelia E. Garrison Waller, having died of natural causes on July 17, 1915, just two months short of her 29th birthday.

"Where were you on Christmas eve night of this past year?" Barnette asked his client.

"Me and my brother Whit took all the kids and rode over to Sarepta to visit with our brother Jesse and his family, it being Christmas time and all," Waller responded.

"And what time did you arrive at your brother's?"

"I don't remember exactly what time we got there. It was probably around 8 o'clock."

"And what did you do after you arrived at your brother's?"

117

"Well, first I fed the horses. The children went on in to supper. I wasn't much hungry 'cause we'd eaten lunch on the way, so I just visited. Soon's we put the boys to bed, me and Jesse went over to Walter's," Waller said, pointing to the man sharing a place at the defense table.

"That's Mr. Walter Dean, your sister's husband?"

"That's right."

"And how long did you stay at the Dean's?"

"Two or three hours at least...we left there...oh, 'bout 11 o'clock."

"And you went directly back to Jesse's?"

"Yes."

"Did you go straight to bed?"

"No. Jennie, that's Jesse's wife, insisted that I eat somethin'—so we sat around and visited, and I ate some fruit. She went on to bed first, and Jesse and me stayed up a little longer."

"Where did you sleep?"

"In a room next to Jesse's with one of the children."

"And you remained there, at your brother's house, the rest of the night?"

"That's right."

"Once you arrived back at your brother's home from Walter Dean's at 11 o'clock Christmas Eve night...did you leave at any time and travel back to Grove?"

"No, sir, I certainly did not. Fact of the matter is, I'd left my shoes and coat in Jesse's room—they'd sure have known if I'd left the house..."

"What time did you get up the next morning?"

"Can't fix the exact time...little before daylight, I suppose...I went back over to Walter's that morning...for a drink...and after that I went into Sarepta for a shave."

At the Prosecution table, Harmon Drew's eyebrows shot up. He scribbled some notes and shoved the notepad over to James M. Foster.

"And after that?" Barnette asked.

"After that we went to the Evergreen school house for a Christmas tree program," Waller continued.

"Mr. Waller, it is some distance from your home in Germantown to your brother's home near Sarepta. What made you decide to make the trip?"

"Well, I had promised a young widow, Mrs. Johnson up in Ward 1, that I would bring her a gift. I'd picked it up at a drug store in Minden...a, uh...one of those things women use to take care of their hands...their nails with..."

"A manicure set?"

"That's it, a manicure set. I had bought it for her and wanted to deliver it myself. I'd already wrote her that I was coming—and I didn't want to disappoint her."

"Mr. Waller, let me ask you this directly....Did you have knowledge of, or did you participate in any way, in the killing of the Reeves family?"

"No, sir, I am absolutely innocent!"

"Thank you, sir. Judge, I tender this witness."

Assistant DA Foster didn't beat around any proverbial bushes.

"Mr. Waller, do you recall being with John Reeves in Minden several days prior to his murder...and his showing you a large roll of money?"

"Objection—the Prosecution has no grounds for this line of questioning!"

"Sustained."

"Sorry," Foster said, his next question proving just the opposite.

"On the Saturday previous to the killings, were you not in Minden inquiring as to the whereabouts of Mark Peters?"

"Was which?" Waller looked confused, as if he didn't understand the question. He was rescued by Barnette, whose objection was again sustained by Judge Sandlin.

"Okay, I'll rephrase the question. Did you not inquire of a certain man in Minden where Mark Peters was?"

"We have already objected to this line of questioning, Judge," Barnette complained loudly.

"Counselor, proceed to another line of questioning."

"Right, sorry sir," Foster nodded, turning back to Waller.

"How long had you lived in Germantown prior to the murders of John Reeves and his family?" he asked, switching gears.

"I moved there about two weeks before Christmas. In fact, I hadn't moved everything from my place in Grove yet."

"Okay, Mr. Waller, let's go back to Sarepta and to your brother's on Christmas Eve night. You say you left your coat and shoes in your brother's room—why, when you slept in another room?"

"Jesse's room had a fire going in it, so I took my coat off there. The room I was in didn't have a fire going...Me 'an Jesse talked awhile and then I went across to another room and went to bed..."

"And the next day, Christmas Day, you rose early...real early...and you rode over to Walter Dean's...for a drink...just after daybreak? Mr. Waller, do you often drink that early in the morning?"

"Objection!"

"Sustained."

"Your honor, I think the defendant's state of mind has relevance here."

"Blaze another path, Mr. Foster..."

"Yes, your honor. You say, Mr. Waller, that you got a shave...on Christmas morning...was it difficult finding a barber open so early on Christmas morning?"

"Objection...Your honor, the Defense takes exception to the Prosecution's accusatory tone and constant battering of Mr. Waller."

"Mr. Foster...please limit your questions to questions...and leave the editorializing off."

"Yes, sir. I do apologize."

He continued questioning the defendant.

"Mr. Waller, you say that Christmas morning, after your drink and after your shave, you rode over to Evergreen to attend a Christmas Tree program, is that right?"

"That's right."

"About what time did you leave your brother's house in Sarepta for the Christmas program in Evergreen?"

"Around noon."

"And what time did you leave Evergreen going back to Sarepta after the program?"

"I'm not sure...it was probably around 10 or so...after the program ended."

"And you rode the same horse over to Evergreen that you rode back to Sarepta later that night?"

120

"That's right."

"And did that long trip...let's see...that would have been about 40 miles...kill the horse?"

Laughter erupted unchecked from the gallery.

Ten-penny nails would have been no match for Judge Sandlin's gavel.

Barnette, red-faced, leaped to his feet and aimed an accusatory finger at Foster, who had managed to pull a most cherubic face.

"Objection...objection!! This is totally uncalled for...Objection!" Barnette hissed.

"I apologize to the honorable defense, your honor," Foster said seraphically, before the gavel-wielding judge could serve up the anticipated reprimand. "But our formidable opponent would compel us to believe that no horse could stand up to the trip from Grove to Sarepta...and quite obviously, the distance from Sarepta to Evergreen and Sarepta to Grove is quite comparable, since Grove and Evergreen and Germantown form a triangle of communities no more than a few miles apart."

"I wouldn't say it was any 20 miles from Sarepta to Evergreen," Waller spat, bringing the focus of the courtroom suddenly convoluting back to the man on the witness stand.

And causing his attorney to cringe noticeably.

Ever an opportunist, Foster jumped on the chance to resume grilling Waller before Judge Sandlin could launch into a tirade concerning the inherent dangers of wreaking havoc on the decorum of his courtroom. The young attorney knew he was very close to being held in contempt.

"Mr. Waller, when did you first learn of the Reeves' murders?"

"Monday night at the Christmas Tree program."

"Did you discuss it with anyone in length?"

"Not really."

"Let me ask you this, Mr. Waller...Tuesday night, after you'd returned home...did you not ring up Sheriff Phillips, and tell him you'd just returned home and that you'd just learned about the killing of the Reeves family? And did you not offer your services in investigating the crime?"

"Judge, we strenuously object to this line of questioning. The basis has not been laid for asking these questions!" Barnette was steamed. "These questions are obviously designed to discredit Mr. Waller and to attack his conduct."

"Judge, we believe that we can show cause for Mr. Waller to answer these questions."

"Gentlemen, let's take a short recess and discuss it," Judge Sandlin said, motioning for all four attorneys to join him. "Mr. Waller, you can step down for the time being."

Henry Waller returned to his seat at the defense table, turned sideways in his chair and stretched his legs, smiling at family members who were seated behind the railing not four feet away. Catching his brother's eye, he put two fingers to his mouth and made like he was smoking. His brother patted his pocket and pulled out a pack of cigarettes and a box of matches. He lit one and handed it to Henry, who took one long drag and exhaled. He winked at his son, who sat squirming on Jennie Waller's lap.

Another of Waller's sons talked animatedly with Cody Reeves, who was pressed against his half-brother's shoulder on the same row. Not three feet away, on a table reserved for physical evidence, lay the ax—its double blades still bearing dried blood and pieces of hair. Neither child seemed to notice it—or to question its existence.

"Mr. Waller, please return to the witness stand, and please remember you're still under oath."

The attorneys stepped aside, leaving Judge Sandlin to pronounce his decision. "As to the admissibility of the question put to Mr. Waller concerning his telephone conversation with Sheriff Phillips, I'm going to allow it. In earlier testimony, the defendant, acting under his own counsel, answered a question relative to his hearing about the Reeves case while he was attending a Christmas program. It's my opinion that this sets precedence for answering the Prosecution's question on this point. I will warn the State, however, that I will not allow questions relative to points not introduced by the defendant or the Defense. You may continue, Mr. Foster."

"Thank you, your honor. Let the court be assured that we ask these questions as a means of testing Mr. Waller's memory and recollection," he said, turning to Waller, "Because, Mr. Waller, if you heard about the murders at the Christmas program Monday night, why then did you call Sheriff Phillips and tell him you had just learned about the killings?"

"Objection...once again, the Prosecution is badgering the witness, your honor," Barnette said.

"You'll have to rephrase your question...or introduce a new line of questioning," Judge Sandlin ruled.

"Mr. Waller, I will ask you whether or not you rang up Sheriff Phillips Tuesday night following Christmas and told him you had been away and had just heard of the Reeves murder and would offer your services?"

"Brother Whit called him up," Waller answered. "When he finished talking to him, I did take the phone."

"Did you tell him you had just gotten back and just heard of the Reeves murder and offer your services?"

"Objection," Barnette chortled.

"Over-ruled, answer the question, Mr. Waller."

"Did you, Mr. Waller?"

"Yes, sir....As a matter of fact, I had heard it at the Christmas Tree, but not any particulars. On the way back home from Sarepta, I met a man who filled me in."

"So why did you tell Sheriff Phillips you had just heard it?"

"I just meant...I just heard it talked about at Evergreen."

"Did Sheriff Phillips tell you that the whole parish was inflamed over the crime?"

"Objection, your honor—that question is purely intended to foster the sentiment of the jury."

"Sustained, move on to another question, Mr. Foster."

"Yes, sir," Foster agreed. "Mr. Waller, you stayed at your brother's in Sarepta until Tuesday morning, is that right?"

"That's right...until Tuesday morning."

"And then you returned to Germantown, just a few miles from the Reeves' place in Grove, right?"

"That's right."

"When you say 'we' you mean your children and who else?"

"My brother Whit and his children."

"Your brother Whit is a preacher of sorts, isn't he?"

"That's right."

"And on Sunday—Christmas eve—he had planned to attend Sunday School and church in Germantown...but you persuaded him to accompany you to Sarepta, is that not right?"

"Objection, your honor."

123

"Over-ruled, I see nothing wrong with the question."

"I didn't know he was going to Sunday School....I didn't know if he was going or not."

"Didn't your brother Whit plan to go to Sarepta on Monday...until you got him to change and go with you?"

"Maybe he was supposed to go on Monday. But I proposed to him that we go on over that evening."

"I've just got one more question—were you drinking on Christmas eve, Mr. Waller?"

"Yes, I was...But I want to say something...I'd like to say why I proposed going over Christmas eve."

Barnette couldn't believe it.....

"Judge, I'd like permission to confer with my client," he said, jumping to his feet.

"I don't blame you," Judge Sandlin said, gesturing permission for Barnette to approach the witness.

"Henry, I'm warning you not to offer anything the Prosecution can use," Barnette rasped. His face was just a few inches from Waller's. "I'm advising you against this, but if you desire to continue, just remember—confine what you say to your explanation—nothing else. Got that?"

"Yeah, I got that."

"Judge, my client wants to complete his statement." He resumed his seat.

"Go ahead, Mr. Waller."

"The reason I wanted to go over to Sarepta on Christmas eve was because there wasn't going to be any womenfolk home to cook...and I was lonesome. Miz Evie was gone and wasn't comin' back til Tuesday. So I figured we could go on over to Jesse's Christmas eve, spend Monday visitin', and get back home Tuesday...same as Evie."

Barnette sighed and swapped pained looks with Robertson. Their client had just opened the door for the Prosecution to ask questions about Eva Anderson's testimony.

They were not disappointed.

"Mrs. Anderson—she's your housekeeper?" Foster asked, his promise of "one more question" all but forgotten.

"You might say that. Evie and her husband and two kids live with me. She does all the cookin' and cleanin'—and they're good company for me 'n my boys. I sure couldn't take care of them four boys by myself."

"I will ask you whether or not Wednesday night while at home and in the presence of Mrs. Anderson you didn't throw your hat on the floor and exclaim with an oath that you wished the whole world would sink?"

"I did not," Waller replied emphatically.

"Didn't you make that statement in substance?"

"No. I didn't throw my hat on the floor—I had just come from the supper table. I mighta told Evie that those Negroes were trying to throw the blame on me..."

"Did you say you wished the whole damned world would sink?"

"I certainly did not."

"Or, if Johnie hadn't talked there'd be nothing to this?"

"No, I did not."

"I will ask again, if on the Saturday previous to the killing you were not in Minden and if you were not inquiring for Mark Peters?"

"Objection...Mr. Foster has already tried this...it's getting old, your honor."

"Sustained."

Foster looked toward Drew. His arched eyebrow posed an unvoiced question...Drew shook his head in response.

"We have no further questions," he said, resuming his seat.

"Then I'll ask you to step down," Judge Sandlin said, gesturing at Waller. "Mr. Barnette...Mr. Robertson...do you want to call another witness?"

"Not at this time, your honor," Barnette replied.

Judge Sandlin, as usual ignoring the clock on the wall, fumbled in his pocket for his timepiece and glanced at it. "It's now 3:30," he said. "We'll take a break and begin rebuttal testimony promptly at 3:45...Court is adjourned."

J.P. Long, recalled by the State as the first rebuttal witness, admitted receiving several letters from his son. They had been written while Johnie was incarcerated in the Caddo jail. The witness couldn't recall the exact dates.

"Did you visit your son in jail at any time?" Foster started the questioning.

"Yes, once."

"And did he tell you about what happened Christmas eve?"

"Objection, your honor—the reasons are self-explanatory."

Judge Sandlin looked thoughtful. He drew a deep breath before responding. "I'm going to allow the statement from Mr. Long in regards to the fact that a statement was made. However, Mr. Foster, Mr. Drew, I'm going to disallow any detailed statement from this witness relating to what was said."

Foster nodded and tried another approach.

"Mr. Long, without going into detail, when you visited your son in jail, did he make a statement to you that was different from the statements he made to you in two letters?"

"Quite different," he replied, before the defense could object.

"Did he tell you what happened on Christmas morning?"

"Yes, he did."

"Did he tell you who was there?"

Barnette could see where Foster was going, and he headed it off. "Your honor, the defense objects to the mentioning of any specific names by this witness."

"Sustained."

Foster continued. "Mr. Long, to your knowledge, did your son make statements to anyone else relative to his whereabouts Christmas eve?"

"He said he talked to Sheriff Hughes and several deputies."

"Do you know what he told them?"

"This is ludicrous, your honor..." Barnette started.

Foster interceded. "Your honor, I was only going to ask Mr. Long whether or not his son told him at any time that the statements he made to the authorities were true or false."

126

"I'll allow the question."

"Mr. Long, did Johnie ever tell you whether or not he made true statements to the authorities?"

"No, sir, he never mentioned if he lied to 'em or told 'em the truth. It just never came up."

Foster contemplated. Somewhat carefully he put forth his next question. "Mr. Long, in the statement your son made to you, did he or did he not say that Henry Waller was present at the killing?"

"Objection!" Barnette was outraged.

Judge Sandlin leaned back and inspected the ceiling. Barnette was still standing, leaning forward with both hands gripping the edge of the defense table.

"I'm going to allow the question," the judge said finally. "But I'm going to instruct Mr. Long to answer the question with a simple 'yes' or 'no' - no explanations."

Barnette looked like he'd been punched in the stomach. He knew arguing was pointless.

Foster beamed. "Well, Mr. Long?"

"Yes."

"He said he was present?"

"Yes."

"Did he tell you Henry Waller took part in the killing?"

"Objection...please!!"

"Over-ruled. Simply answer the question, Mr. Long."

"Well, Mr. Long," Foster arched his eyebrows, "Did he?"

"Yes, sir, he did."

****

Long was dismissed.

Foster's adrenaline was pumping.

He walked to the prosecution table and picked up an envelope.

"Your honor, if the court will allow, we'd like to offer at this time a second letter from Johnie Long to his father that was introduced earlier...but that the defense failed to bring to the jury...Mr. Robertson himself introduced the letters...and read one to this court...but he failed to read the second one."

Foster's accusatory tone failed to ruffle the two defense attorneys.

"Judge," Barnette argued, "of course both letters were introduced, and the jury has every right to read them. But this particular letter is in great detail and we chose not to read it because of its length."

Judge Sandlin motioned for Foster to bring him the letter. He peered at it in his familiar manner—over the top of his spectacles.

"I would concur with Mr. Barnette," he said, pursing his lips. "Let's not take any more of this court's valuable time in reading another detailed letter. We should have faith that the jury will make a point of reading the letter during deliberations."

Foster sneaked a quick look at Drew and shrugged his shoulders.

****

The prosecutors were given virtually free reign in the questioning of Caddo Parish Sheriff Hughes as rebuttal testimony continued. The State would ask a question, the defense would object, the judge would over-rule.

Hughes repeated his testimony about the arrest of Johnie Long on Thursday, December 28 and his confession as he was being driven from Grove to Shreveport.

Once more he told the court how Mark Peters had confessed to him in his jail earlier that Thursday. He told about Chester Tyson's refusal to admit taking part in the crime until his removal to the Texarkana jail and his subsequent confession to hired private investigator Will Lloyd.

"Didn't Chester Tyson originally place the time of the killings at 12 o'clock, and then later he changed his testimony to 1:30 or 2 o'clock?" defense attorney Robertson asked on cross.

"That's correct."

"Did that not strike you as odd?"

"Not really—most people can't fix a time when they're forced to...for all we knew, he couldn't even tell time."

No one could argue that.

Time and time again Hughes denied that he or any of his deputies coerced, threatened, or intimidated any of the suspects.

Caddo Deputy D.D. Bazer, taking the stand for the first time, also denied using threats. He recalled how Mark Peters had confessed to him on Thursday following the murders. He remembered the times varying and agreed with his boss that this was not unusual in a criminal investigation.

Clyde Toadvin, the Minden chauffeur who drove the officers and Johnie Long from Grove to Shreveport, backed up their stories about the absence of threats and promises.

Private investigator Teddy Price had heard Tyson's confession in his office after the Negro originally spilled his guts to the undercover PI. He placed the time of the murders at several hours after midnight then—and during his trial.

"Mr. Price, you are a paid investigator, are you not? And you were hired by Webster Parish to help investigate the Reeves murder, is that right?" Robertson asked on cross.

Price's normally pale cheeks flushed primrose. The rosy color contrasted starkly with the detective's carrot-colored hair, making his reaction all the more obvious. But he held his temper in check, even to his own surprise.

"That's correct. My brother and I own and operate the Price Detective Agency. We were hired to assist with the initial investigation."

"What was your fee?"

"Five dollars a day."

"And how many days did you work?"

"Twenty days."

"Mr. Price, do you remember having a conversation with the mayor of Minden several days after the trial of the four Negroes already convicted in this case?"

"Not precisely...I've had hundreds of conversations during the course of this case."

"Let me refresh your memory. You told the mayor that— based on your investigation—you didn't believe Henry Waller was present at the killings."

"Your honor," Drew objected. "Who's testifying here—Mr. Robertson or Mr. Price?"

"If you have a question for this witness, ask it, Mr. Robertson," the judge responded.

"Do you remember telling the mayor that?"

"I told a lot of people a lot of things," Price fidgeted. "Often you tell people what they want to hear because you haven't got time to argue...you've got other business to attend to...so you tell 'em what they want to hear and get on with the job."

"So you deny telling the mayor that Henry Waller wasn't there?"

"No, I'm not denying that I told him that."

Robertson smiled. Price stewed.

"Do you remember accompanying Anderson Heard, who is now incarcerated in the State penitentiary for the Reeves murders, to the scene of the crime the day he confessed?"

"Yes, I do."

"And do you remember a conversation you had with the deputy who accompanied you relative to Heard's telling of the facts and how you could better relate to the crime through Heard's description of it...do you remember that conversation?"

"Like I've already said, I've had hundreds of conversations..."

"Do you remember saying that Heard's story matched the physical facts? And do you recall that Heard denied that Waller was involved...?"

"Not specifically."

"Do you remember trying to get Heard to say that white men were involved...to convince Heard that things would go better for him if he pointed a finger at white men?"

"I certainly did not."

"Oh! Suddenly you remember this particular conversation."

"I remember asking Anderson Heard if white men, and, yes, maybe if Henry Waller, were involved in the killings. I certainly did not advise the man that things would go lighter for him if he implicated anyone. That's preposterous!"

"No more questions." Robertson dismissed Price with a flash of his hand. He mildly disliked this witness and held no fear of showing it.

But Foster was already rising to the challenge, bent on repairing any damage through re-examination. He walked over and stood in front of the jury.

"Mr. Price, didn't you, in fact, try to get Tyson and Peters to say that Henry Waller was NOT at the murder and that one of them used the ax?"

"That's right."

"And they refused?"

"That's right."

"Isn't it true, that during the course of a grueling investigation, people ask you hundreds of questions?"

"Hundreds."

"And do you take the time to specifically answer all of these questions?"

"No, that would be impossible. I just try to mollify who I'm talking too without angering them or endearing them to me. Most times I don't even know what angle they're interested in, so I give 'em a quick answer and go about the business of solving a case. That's my priority."

"So you might say something that you think the person wants to hear just to - for the lack of a better description - get them off your back?"

"Exactly."

"Thank you, Mr. Price."

Foster walked back to his seat at the Prosecution table.

"We'd like to call Ardis Taylor to the stand now, your honor."

Taylor was called and sworn.

"Mr. Taylor, this past Sunday - at the request of the District Attorney - you rode a horse from the Reeves cabin in Grove to the home of Jesse Waller in Sarepta, and back, didn't you?"

Foster remained seated. He didn't want the jury to be distracted by his presence - wanted them to be able to compute in their own heads the figures his witness was going to produce.

"I sure did," Ardis Taylor answered.

"Would you tell us about it."

"Be glad to," he said, remembering.......

****

Ardis Taylor shrugged off a shiver and reined in his horse. Fog was just beginning its dawn retreat from the dark, fast-flowing waters of the narrow, meandering Bayou Dorcheat. It played tricks on his eyes as he strained to watch out for Drew and his entourage.

In fact, engine noise from an approaching automobile signaled the arrival of the district attorney. Taylor's horse snorted and pawed at the ground as the car approached. He skillfully quieted the jumpy animal, clucking his tongue and pulling masterfully on the rein, tightening the bit. He couldn't blame the horse for being skittish - he felt kinda spooky himself.

131

He was flattered that Mr. Drew had asked him to re-enact Henry Waller's now famous (albeit alleged) ride from the Reeves' cabin in Grove to the Waller's house in Sarepta, and back.

Problem was, the bayou here at Knuckles Ford was high. This was the way Waller would a gone, 'cause it was the shortest way over the bayou to Sarepta.

So Drew was meeting him and they would work something out.

Drew emerged from the car - a youngish, portly man in a three-piece suit who looked out of place in the dewy, earthy smelling woods. Taylor noticed the way he walked back on his heels, never looking down, always looking you in the eye.

"Ardis," Drew proffered his hand and Taylor shook it. "What do you think about it?"

"Well, sir, looks like the water ain't gonna retreat any time soon. There's lots a difference, you know, in this old bayou in December 'n March. Been a good bit a rain here and on up in Arkansas last coupla days, ya know."

"Well, how much out of the way would it be to take the Sikes Ferry route?"

"Now 'ats an idea -- be further, prob'ly six miles or so. Want me to try it?"

"Yes - this testimony is essential...and if you can make the trip with even a greater distance to ride...more power to us. Yes - let's do it."

"You got it, sir. I'll ride 'er first thing in the morning."

****

James Foster didn't hurry Taylor through the story-telling, letting him describe in detail the pony ride through pathways first hacked out by Indians who considered the scenic "Dauchite" bayou as their lifeblood.

Soon, automobiles would require wider, less bumpy roadways.

"How many miles did you ride?" Foster asked when Taylor finished.

"Well, sir, like I said, the bayou was high there where I'd a normally crossed - at Knuckles Ford - so I went on up to the Sikes crossing. That'd be about 60 miles...for the round trip."

"When did you leave the Reeves' place?"

"Right at 10:30 in the mornin' - had to take care of my livestock and feed my face."

Taylor chuckled. Foster smiled. He liked an undaunted witness.

"And what time did you arrive back at the Reeves?"

"It was 'bout 5 o'clock."

"That's six and a half hours for the entire trip. Did you stop and rest after you got to Sarepta?"

"Yes, sir, I took me a lunch and stopped for, oh, not quite an hour."

"Now, sir, you say you rode via Sikes Ferry...and that's longer than the Knuckles Ford route?"

"Oh, yes sir....it's longer by a good eight miles."

"That's eight miles both ways - sixteen miles longer altogether?"

"That's right."

"So, what you're essentially saying is that you rode from the Reeves home in Grove to the Waller home in Sarepta and then back to the Reeves' home in less than five and a half hours, going 16 miles out of your way?"

"You got it figured right."

"Had your horse been ridden any other distances that day?"

"Sure, rode it from Minden to Grove...then back home agin...that's probly 'bout 15 mile. Guess I rode 'im 'bout 75 mile altogether."

"No more questions for this witness, your honor."

He looked at the Defense table. Robertson stood up.

"Is your horse an unusually good horse for long distances, Mr. Taylor?" Robertson asked, walking toward the witness.

"Can't say as he is...ordinary cow pony...bought him from Dr. Taber for $35," Taylor answered.

"Thank you," he said, dismissing Taylor with a wave of his hand and reclaiming his seat.

Foster next called W. W. Simpson, a reputable horse trader from Minden. Simpson testified that he had easily ridden seven and a half or eight miles in less than an hour without being in a big hurry. In fact, he said, a good horse could fox trot that gait.

"And would that horse be worth $1,000?" Robertson had asked bitingly.

"Can't say that it would," Simpson had responded, non-plussed. "Any average country horse can travel eight miles an hour."

Sam Grant, a stockman in Webster Parish, testified that the Knuckles Ford route from the Reeves' home to Sarepta was 18 miles, and that a man could ride it, round trip, in four hours or less.

"Why, I knew a man who rode from Shreveport to Wascom, Texas - that's 20 miles - in two hours. Any man who's familiar with an area can ride 18 to 20 miles in two hours without any problem," Grant said.

"Are you familiar with any of the Waller's horses?" Foster asked.

"Pretty much. In fact, Waller's got one real healthy horse I know about."

"Are you familiar with the horse described by Johnie Long?"

"Sure am...Fact I brought it from Texas...it's a black, real gentle five-year-old."

Robertson didn't attempt to ask Grant about horses. He elected, instead, to launch an off-hand, personal attack.

"Mr. Grant, before you became an 'expert' stockman, you were a police officer in Shreveport, were you not?"

"That's right."

"But you are no longer a police officer?"

"No, sir. I lost my job when the new administration took over."

Robertson cocked his head to one side and looked at the witness thoughtfully.

"No more questions, your honor."

"Hutch" Phillips returned to the stand next. Foster continued the questioning.

"Sheriff Phillips, earlier in this trial, Henry Waller testified that on the Wednesday following the murders, at his home in the presence of Mrs. Eva Anderson, he became very upset because he had, and I quote, 'been informed that the Negroes had implicated him' in the Reeves murders. I asked him specifically if that event took place Wednesday night...and he said, yes, he was sure it was Wednesday night?"

Foster paused for the jury to ingest what he had just said.

"Sheriff, when did you and your deputies learn about the Negroes implicating Mr. Waller?"

"Thursday. None of my deputies knew anything about the accusations until I personally went over to Shreveport Thursday afternoon and heard the confessions for myself. They wouldn't have known anything about it until later that night...when we came back over to Minden to have warrants issued."

"Thank you, Sheriff."

Robertson rose and stood before Sheriff Phillips.

"Sheriff, you have a deputy named Milam Miller, don't you?"

"Yes."

"Well, if Mr. Waller said that Deputy Miller told him on Wednesday that the Negroes had implicated him in the killings, could we trust your deputy?"

"Milam Miller is a reputable man, if that's what you're asking, but he couldn't possi..."

"Thank you, Sheriff Phillips."

"But, he couldn't...."

"That's all, Sheriff Phillips...you answered the question quite satisfactorily," Robertson said. He turned his back to Phillips, walked to his seat, sat down, and busied himself scribbling notes.

Judge Sandlin leaned towards Phillips, who had remained seated, stewing over Robertson's refusal to let him finish his statement. He motioned for him to draw closer. The two men conferred in whispers for several seconds. Sheriff Phillips then stepped down from his seat, and walked to the rail dividing the audience from the bench. Behind him, Judge Sandlin slipped quietly from the courtroom.

"As you can see, it is now 6 o'clock," the sheriff said. "Judge Sandlin has ordered a one-hour break. The jury will be retired to chambers during this time for supper. I will warn you right now, that if you leave your seats for any reason, you may not have them when you return—and standing will not be allowed in this courtroom. So take your chances."

With that, Phillips motioned for the members of the jury to follow him, which they did eagerly.

****

The courtroom came suddenly to life. No one wanted to leave, and everyone wanted to talk. Dinner took a back seat to

135

conversation. A few people looked uncomfortable, as they mentally weighed their desire to stay versus their need to visit the nearest water closet.

At least one spectator figured a way around the hunger issue. He lowered a string from the second floor window to someone waiting below. One tug later, and he was hoisting up a sack of boiled egg sandwiches. This set off a "string" of copycat deliveries.

****

Fresh from the one-hour break, Harmon Drew wasted no time recalling Johnie Long to the stand as the first rebuttal witness. He grabbed a letter from the evidence table and handed it to the youthful witness.

"Johnie, do you recognize this letter?"

"Yes, sir."

"Is it one of two letters you wrote to your father while you were incarcerated in Caddo Parish?"

"Yes, sir."

"Your honor," Robertson half rose and addressed the judge. "I don't know where Mr. Drew is going with these questions, but please remind him that you have already ruled concerning the reading of this letter in open court."

"Mr. Robertson...I don't think I need to be told how to run my court." Judge Sandlin's voice mirrored a rebuke. "And I feel sure that Mr. Drew's memory will not fail him in this matter. Proceed, counselor."

"Thank you, sir," Drew hastily continued, non-plussed by Robertson's obloquy. "Now, Johnie, I'll ask you to read this letter - to yourself."

Long glanced down at the letter and began reading...his lips quietly and slowly mouthing the words. When he was finished, his eyes sought Drew, who took the letter from the youth's hands.

"This was the second letter entered into evidence by the defense," he said, returning it to the table and turning back to his witness.

"Johnie, you wrote that letter, didn't you?"

"Yes, sir, you know that."

"Johnie, in that letter you just read - the letter that you wrote to your father from jail - did you connect that man sitting there..." he turned and pointed to Henry Waller... "did you connect

136

him with the killings of the Reeves family on Christmas eve night?"

"Objection!" Robertson and Barnette barked concurrently.

Drew shook his head. "What possible objection could you have to this question? The letter has been admitted—presented by you. Judge Sandlin has ruled that the jury can read the letter...what possible objection can you have?"

"It's grand-standing," Robertson bellowed.

"And you recognize it as such?" Drew retorted, mocking surprise.

"Gentlemen, that's enough," Sandlin rapped his gavel but once. "I'm going to allow Mr. Long to answer the question...then we'll proceed to something else...gentlemen."

"I'll repeat my question, Johnie," he turned back to Long, who had watched the volley of words in wide-eyed bewilderment. "In the letter you just read, did you connect Henry Waller to the Reeves murders?"

"I did."

"Thank you, Johnie. Now let me ask you another question. Do you know Benjamin Wrenn?"

"Yes, sir, I do."

"This morning, Benjamin Wrenn told this court under oath that he visited with Chester Tyson just moments after he left this very stand on Wednesday." Drew patted the arm of the witness chair for emphasis. "He told this court that Chester Tyson told him that he wasn't near the Reeves place on Christmas eve night...that he slept over with Anderson Heard."

Drew was just getting warmed up.

"Do you also know that, according to Mr. Wrenn, Chester Tyson said in the same conversation—mind you not minutes after he testified here in this court about his part in the killings—he told Mr. Wrenn that he didn't know who committed the murders?"

Drew was looking at the jury as he talked. Feigning an incredulous look, he suddenly turned back to Long.

"You wouldn't have happened to be in the same room with Mr. Wrenn when he had his visit with Mr. Tyson, would you have?"

"Guess so, sir. I saw Ben in the grand jury room right after Chester's testimony Wednesday even'n."

"Was anybody else there?"

137

"Sure - Deputy Bell, Mr. Hardy, Mark Peters...and 'course Chester was there."

"What did Mr. Wrenn say?"

"He just tole Deputy Bell he wanted to speak to the negras."

"And did he?"

"He shook hands with 'em and asked 'em how they was doin'...then he asked Chester if he was really at that killin'."

"And what did Chester say?" Drew stepped towards the jury box as he asked the question. He carefully watched the faces of each juror as Long gave his answer.

"He told him he was."

"You mean Chester *didn't* tell Benjamin Wrenn that he wasn't involved in the murders...that he knew nothing about the killings?"

"No, sir. Chester didn't deny nothin' 'bout what he said in court that day."

"No more questions, your honor. But let me warn the Defense that if the State decides to pursue charges of perjury against Mr. Wrenn...and the Defense wants to argue that it is a case of self-incrimination or hearsay....we are prepared to bring more witnesses to the stand to substantiate what Mr. Long has told us...including Deputy C.J. Bell."

"Do you have any questions or comments, Mr. Robertson...Mr. Barnette?" Judge Sandlin looked sharply from one man to the other.

"No, sir," Robertson answered.

"Good," Judge Sandlin said coolly. "Mr. Drew, does the State want to call any more rebuttal witnesses?"

"We do not, sir."

He returned his gaze to the defense team.

Robertson nodded affirmatively. "We'd like to call Dave Frazier at this time."

While the bailiff was getting Frazier, Drew asked the court's permission to enter a government soil survey map into evidence. According to the map, the distance from the Reeves place in Grove to Sarepta by air was 14 miles.

****

Frazier, a young man making his first trip to the witness stand, was sworn.

"Mr. Frazier, you accompanied Detective Ted Price, Deputy Milam Miller, and Ardis Taylor to the Reeves home with the convicted Negro Anderson Heard shortly after the Negro confessed, didn't you?" Robertson asked, walking over to stand in front of the jury.

"Yes, sir."

"Did you hear Detective Price tell the Negro that it would be better for him, that the law would deal more lightly with him, if he swore that white men - specifically Henry Waller - were involved in the crime?"

"Yes, sir."

Robertson remained facing the jury.

"And, sir, at that time, did Anderson Heard admit that Henry Waller was there and that he took part in the killing of the Reeves family?"

"No, sir, he didn't. The Negro told Mr. Price that Mr. Waller was not there."

Robertson continued staring at the jury.

"We have no more questions, your honor."

His honor looked at Drew.

"The People's case has been presented," Drew said.

Judge Sandlin nodded.

"In that case, court will recess for 15 minutes. Closing arguments will begin at precisely 8:45. Gentlemen..."

****

"Motive and opportunity, gentlemen. That's what this trial boils down to - motive and opportunity."

Robertson looked smug as he approached the jury box.

"Let's talk about motive.

Gentlemen of the jury, the State would have you believe that Henry Waller, a prominent citizen of this parish, would butcher, in cold blood, an entire family because he was afraid someone was going to 'tattle' on him.

Tattle on him for what? Just what was this awful deed? What was this deed that was so vile that a family man and prominent citizen felt forced to kill a friend...and his entire family...to suppress it? Has the Prosecution, at any time during this trial, told us? No, of course not. Because there was no such thing. This 'motive' exists only in the mind of a man trying to save

139

his own neck—this motive exists solely in the mind of the Prosecution's star witness - Johnie Long.

There is no motive!

But the Prosecution would have you believe that Henry Waller, a man with four young children, would brutally murder in the most cold-blooded of ways, three small children as they slept. Why? Because he hated their father? Was their father not a man he played cards with...and drank with...and socialized with?

There is no motive.

You've observed Henry Waller in this courtroom. Does he strike you as a cold-blooded killer? You've watched him with his children. Do they shrink from him? No, they climb upon his lap...they love him.

Think about it. Does what the State want you to believe sound unbelievable? Does it? Because it is!!

Now, let's look at the Prosecution's key witnesses.

Chester Tyson is a convicted killer. He's going to hang for the murders of the Reeves family because he admitted taking part in the killings. At one time he tells us everything happened at 11 o'clock...then he tells us 12 midnight...then he tells us after midnight. He tells us Mark Peters, also convicted and sentenced to hang, lied to us during his testimony. Chester Tyson was going to get married on Christmas day. What better motive to rob and kill John Nelson Reeves? Is it not more probable that Chester Tyson heard rumors of Reeves' collecting money from his wife's inheritance...knew he would need money for a wife and new family...and decided to rob the man he despised? He admitted he'd been drinking that night. Wouldn't it be more likely that a combination of alcohol, and greed, and hate would lead to murder?

*But there's more. Anderson Heard, who is serving a life sentence for his part in the murders, says he slept over at Chester's Christmas Eve night. And he told this very court that his friend, Chester, **used the ax that killed the Reeves family**. He told us that Henry Waller wasn't there! And do you know who he told this to first? Detective Teddy Price - a paid employee and witness for the State!*

Then, we must consider the star witness in this case— Johnie Long—an impressionable young man who has already admitted his guilt...An impressionable young man who wants to blame someone besides himself for his participation in this heinous crime. We know by his own admission that he took part in the murders along with the four other men who have been tried, convicted, and sentenced. Two of those...to death. We know by the letters to his father that he will lie to save face. What then, gentlemen, will he do to save his own neck? Will he lie? Will he blame someone else? Will he make a deal? You bet he will!

To have murder, you must have motive. Gentlemen, the State has failed to prove that there was motive in this case.

So, what about opportunity?

Henry Waller spent Christmas night with his family - in Sarepta - at least 20 miles from the scene of the crime. That is a fact. A virtual parade of witnesses told of seeing the Waller family on their way to Sarepta.

Some of the most outstanding citizens of this parish testified to seeing Henry Waller at various times in and around Sarepta on Christmas eve night - and early Christmas morning. Little Thomas Waller told this court that he heard his father, aunt and uncle getting the Christmas presents ready on Christmas eve after they had returned from visiting relatives. That would have to have been close to midnight. Then, before daylight, the household is up again. And we all know how early children rise on Christmas morning, don't we?

So, the Prosecution would have you believe that Mr. Waller used the five hours between midnight and 5 a.m. to commit the most heinous crime of the century.

Don't you think that Mr. Waller's alibi lends itself to more than a reasonable doubt as to his innocence? What the Prosecution wants you to swallow is a conspiracy, gentlemen...A conspiracy involving a very, very tight timeframe. Would not Mr. Waller have had to make at least one trial run in order to carry off a crime of this magnitude - to make sure that it would work? There has been no evidence introduced to that point. And what about all the contingencies. We're talking Christmas Eve, gentlemen...a time when families gather together, and celebrate, and play Santa Claus until the wee hours of the morning...and arise early with their excited children. Could there be a worse night of the year to plan a daring murder miles and miles away?

Common sense tells us the answer to that question.

141

Does this not lend itself to more than a reasonable doubt, gentlemen? A reasonable doubt. If you have even the slightest doubt as to Mr. Waller's guilt, you must find him innocent.

Take a step back and look. Are you convinced, beyond a reasonable doubt, that Henry Waller could ride a horse from his brother's home in Sarepta to Grove, 20 miles away, gather up his co-conspirators, walk to the Reeves home, murder five people, divide up the spoils, and return to his brother's house back in Sarepta - all between the hours of midnight and 5 a.m.? Are you? I know I'm not. I'm not even convinced that Mr. Waller would dream such a thing were possible. Surely you must entertain a reasonable doubt as to Mr. Waller's even daring such a trip.

Lastly, but far from least importantly, where's the evidence?

Where's the evidence linking Henry Waller to the crime?

The State is expecting you to believe that a man could commit bloody mayhem - and yet not have one single drop of blood on his person, his clothes, the saddle of his horse, his shoes...Where's the cold hard evidence?

There is no evidence. The murder weapon did not belong to Henry Waller...was not found anywhere near Henry Waller. Items stolen from the Reeves household were not recovered on Mr. Waller nor his property.

No money has been recovered.

Where is the evidence linking Henry Waller to the crime?

It doesn't exist because Henry Waller did not conspire to carry out, nor did he carry out, this most horrible of crimes.

Gentlemen, the State has produced no evidence.

The State has not proved motive.

The State has not proved opportunity.

What they have proved is that Mr. Waller, an outstanding citizen of this parish, has been framed in the most horrible of ways. By friends. By employees - people he helped and trusted.

Mr. Waller loves children. Heavens...he has four young children of his own. Children who obviously adore him. He loved his wife. He would never harm a child or a mother. He is innocent.

And it is your duty to find him so.

Thank you, Gentlemen.

****

Harmon Drew passed his hand over his eyes, pushed back his chair, and rose to his feet. He walked confidently to the jury box, deliberately locking eyes with first one, then another, of the jurors.

Then he began.

"You know what I find interesting? I find the Defense's decision to attack the State's witnesses very interesting. I mean, under no coercion, did Johnie Long confess to the murders of the Reeves family in the presence of several respected law enforcement officers on the very night he was arrested? Yes. Did he implicate the defendant, Henry Waller, at that time? Yes. Did he really ever change his story? No. Earlier in this trial, did he again testify about Henry Waller's part in the killings? Yes. Did he have anything to gain? No.

Chester Tyson and Mark Peters...did they both testify that Henry Waller master-minded and carried out the killings of the Reeves family? Yes. Having been tried, convicted, and sentenced to hang...did they have anything to gain by implicating Mr. Waller? No.

The Defense has wasted your time in its attempts to discredit these witnesses.

...Motive.

When Johnie Long says that Henry Waller wanted to 'take care of John Reeves because he 'knew something on him' and was going to use it for gain, why should we doubt him? Then there's the rumors of the Reeves having come into some money. And at least two key witnesses admitted that Waller had convinced them to relieve Mr. Reeves of that money. Maybe Henry Waller wanted to shut Mr. Reeves up permanently. Maybe he wanted to rob him and was caught in the act. So he butchered the witnesses.

Motive is, after all, an elusive thing.

Would you agree that what might drive one man to murder might drive another to the bottle? What might make one man mean might make another saintly? What might make one man weak might make another man strong? What drives a man to murder? Do we know? Can we know? Can we know the demons that possess a man's soul?

143

Consider all these questions...and then look at the evidence that proves without a shadow of a doubt that Henry Waller masterminded and carried out a most heinous crime.

Gentlemen, motive pales to insignificance in the presence of madness.

The Defense would have you believe that their client and victim John Reeves were close friends. You know better. True, he socialized with John Reeves. But gambling with a man and drinking his whiskey does not constitute friendship. More than one witness told this court that John Reeves and Henry Waller were antagonists...at the most, unfriendly acquaintances. Neither trusted the other. Their families did not socialize. Their association was fueled by a common need of liquor, gambling, and carousing. This was hardly a basis for a warm, friendly relationship.

More than one witness testified as to the character of Mr. Waller—how he threatened innocent children and stole from his own family. Yet, the Defense would have you believe that Mr. Waller was a model citizen.

But evidence points to the contrary. The Defense has bombarded you with a seemingly endless parade of witnesses, testifying to the good character of the defendant. A close look at most of them reveals a connection to Mr. Waller or his family in some way. And what family won't protect its own? Would not their love for their brother, and uncle...cloud their judgment? This is noble. And this is normal. But is this the truth?

Could Henry Waller tell the difference between truth...and lies? Or, did he lie so often that he sometimes forgot what story he'd told.

He gives us, on three different occasions, three different reasons for going to Sarepta on Christmas eve.

First, he says he went to visit a "special" lady - he had a gift for her. He even told us that it was a manicure set. At the next opportunity, though, he tells us that he went to Sarepta because he had not seen his sister in a long time. Yet he seems to spend his time there doing very little visiting with her. And finally, he tells us that the reason he went to Sarepta was because there were no womenfolk left at home to cook him a warm Christmas meal.

And what about opportunity?

Would these same people stretch hours into minutes for the sake of a loved one? Would they hedge on the time he went to bed?

144

The time he rose in the morning? Expert after expert testified that it is entirely possible for a man to ride from Sarepta to Grove within a five-hour time limit. The opportunity was there, gentlemen.

Would these same people look beyond the bad and, out of love, see him as a good man? A good father? Would they close their eyes to his problem with drink? Would they justify it somehow in their minds? Of course they would. Maybe we'd do the same thing.

But in fact, Henry Waller was not a kind man, nor a tolerant man, nor a principled man. He woke up drinking and he went to bed drinking. Who can testify as to his state of mind on Christmas eve night? Had he been drinking all day? You can be pretty sure of that. Did he not have another drink before breakfast Christmas morning? He admitted to us that he had.

Maybe Henry Waller didn't have a totally black heart. And then again, maybe he did. Maybe Henry Waller didn't go to the Reeves home to murder anyone. But his purpose in going there was far from noble. And when he got there, something snapped. He became a monster...a monster driven by a demon...driven by poison...driven by alcohol. He tendered control of his mind and soul to alcohol, gentlemen. And innocent people...innocent babies...paid the price.

You know, maybe....just maybe....Henry Waller doesn't even remember being there...doesn't even remember wielding the ax that killed five people.

But can we excuse Henry Waller because of his weakness? The Law says we cannot. You know in your hearts we cannot. No, it is our duty to remind him of what he did...and the penalty he has to pay - his life for their lives. He...is...responsible...for the deaths...of five people! The blood of John Reeves...and Maud Reeves...and David Reeves...and Woodrow Reeves...and tiny Alto Reeves...is on his hands. And he must be found accountable. And he must be made to pay the price.

And you....must see...that he does.

Friday, March 16, 1917
Webster Parish Courthouse
Minden, Louisiana

Hutch Phillips leaned back and stretched one, then the other, of his gangly legs across the top corner of his massive desk. Ignoring the stacks of papers, over-flowing ashtrays, and stained coffee cups, he lit a fresh cigarette and inhaled deeply.

Fifteen minutes earlier, his deputies had taken Henry Waller from the courtroom back to his cell.

Closing arguments the night before had begun shortly after 8 o'clock and had taken nearly four hours. Another 25 minutes for Judge Sandlin to deliver the charge had pushed the beginning of jury deliberations to well after midnight. The judge had waited around for about 15 minutes before taking himself home.

When court reconvened at 9 a.m., the jury had been out for nine hours.

Hopeful tension surged through the room when the 12 men responsible for deciding Waller's fate returned to the courtroom shortly after nine. But foreman J.E. Farrar simply asked the judge to repeat his instructions relating to the different verdicts allowed. The jurors then went back to their deliberations and rumors of a mistrial swept the courthouse.

Phillips tilted his hat back and stared vacantly at the ceiling. He feared a mistrial, too. A quick verdict almost always meant a conviction. The longer a jury stayed out, the better the chances for an acquittal.

As if taking his queue from the sheriff's thoughts, Deputy Watts suddenly appeared in the doorway.

"Takin' their goddamn time about it," he said, grabbing a chair and straddling it with bowed legs. The sheriff was more than his boss, he was his friend. Neither minded the other's company.

"Well, if Mr. Waller gets off, we've got those three other counts against him," Phillips said. "Eventually, we'll get him. We'll turn this parish upside down for evidence if we have to...but we'll get him."

Watts took aim at the tin can he was carrying and projected a missile of brown spit deftly toward it. Bulls eye! One thing the boss didn't tolerate was spittin' snuff or tobacco into a good cup or onto the floor. In the old jail, it had been different.

"Interestin' how Drew threw in the possibility of Henry being so liquored up he didn't remember doing it, wasn't it?" Watts half-commented, half-asked.

"Well, if you don't look at the evidence or listen to any witnesses, Waller's pretty convincing. If he's convinced himself he didn't do it - he doesn't have to put on an act."

"Yeah, but can you imagine what has to be going through his head? I mean, you black out - you can't remember - and you listen to all these people accusing you of a God-awful crime. No...I don't buy it. I think he planned it. He may have had a black out - boozin' up to get the courage to do it - but he planned it, sure as I'm sittin' here."

Hutch Phillips made no comment.

"Heard they've already taken one vote," Watts continued. "Heard it was six for hangin', four for life, and two for acquittal— can you believe that? How can anybody with half a brain think that joker's innocent?"

Hutch Phillips sighed. Watts wasn't going to shut up, so he might as well join the conversation.

"You know some folks aren't going to admit that a white man could be capable of this kind of thing," he said. "They'd rather think that all negras are animals and blame everything on 'em. You know those boys on that jury know that the negras have already been convicted. So, they're probably arguing that hanging the negras will be enough...And that Waller's from too good a family to ever do anything like that."

"Yeah, but we know better, don't we?"

"Yeah, but we see a lot of things most folks don't...we know there's no such thing as anyone being 'above' the law. And...they don't think about the fact that all bad people come from regular families - most times good families...good people...families who love 'em. It's not the family's fault when someone goes bad. Sometimes it's just that person's nature. And the family gets hurt the most."

"Yeah, but that don't give a family a right to close their eyes to that person's faults and to take up for 'em no matter what."

"No, but most times they do...who knows, we might do the same thing."

"I damn sure hope not."

"Let's hope we never have to find out."

147

It was 4 o'clock in the afternoon.

The jury had returned.

Judge Sandlin had been handed the verdict, and, in the minds of many courthouse observers, he was taking his own sweet time reading it.

Finally, he looked up.

If he felt any compassion for the defendant who was awaiting his fate - his slow, deliberate movements and solemn demeanor failed to show it.

He handed the papers back to the bailiff, who handed them to Mr. Farrar. Protocol demanded that he ask the jury if they had reached a verdict.

"We have, your honor," Farrar stated. His hands trembled slightly.

"Then please rise and deliver it, sir," the judge instructed.

Farrar, a railroad switch man not accustomed to so much attention, blushed and rose to his feet. He cleared his throat.

"In the matter of the State versus Henry M. Waller, we, the jury find the defendant guilty of murder without capital punishment."

Waller's sister wailed and fell back onto the hard court bench, sobbing uncontrollably into her hands.

Waller had risen while the verdict was being read. Now he half-turned toward his sister, than sank down into his own chair, his mouth open, his face registering disbelief.

Pencils flew across notepads as reporters transposed the scene around them to written word. And as the noise level in the frenzied courtroom began to escalate, Judge Sandlin fired off a few rounds with his gavel.

"I'll have order," he bellowed. "Order, now!"

The spontaneous, emotional babble stopped abruptly, magnifying the disquieting sounds of a woman sobbing. Judge Sandlin looked directly at Henry Waller.

"Please rise, Mr. Waller," he barked, and waited for the guilty man to stand. "Before I sentence you, is there any statement you'd like to make as to why the penalty as defined by law should not be imposed upon you?"

"I'm innocent," Waller's voice cracked. "I don't deserve this, none of this. I didn't kill them people! I've been framed - you'll see."

"You'll see," he repeated, looking at the jury.

"Mr. Waller, you've been found guilty of the charge of murder without capital punishment by a jury of your peers. As the law sets forth, I sentence you to spend the remainder of your natural life incarcerated at the Louisiana State Penitentiary at Angola."

T. W. Robertson finally spoke.

"Judge, on behalf of my client, I'd like to petition this court for a new trial."

"Denied," Sandlin said flatly.

"Then, your honor, we'll carry our appeal to the highest courts in the land."

"Carry it wherever you want, Mr. Robertson. But remember, your client has several other charges pending against him. Another jury might not be as generous with his life."

Sandlin picked up his gavel.

"This court is dismissed."

He brought the gavel down.

"Sheriff, remove this man from my courtroom."

If the word "tidy" was in the dictionary, Thomas Wafer Fuller had never stumbled across it. And as a man who made his living from words, he visited Daniel Webster's famous tome quite frequently.

The small cubbyhole where the editor and owner of the *Webster Signal* worked - lived - was crammed with papers and books. There were old newspapers, an atlas or two, yellowed tablets bearing hurriedly scratched notes (legible only to him while they were still warm), wads of discarded trash...small pieces, big pieces. Trash containers were a waste of good money - something valuable might get accidentally thrown away!

For a newspaper man, anything resembling paper could, and often did at a moment's notice, become the medium on which the story of a lifetime began to take shape. Fancy gift wrap could hold the future of the next Joseph Pulitzer.

Right now, Fuller sat hunched over his typewriter, a Smith Premiere, his most prized possession in the world. He was oblivious to the stale haze of tobacco smoke that perpetually hung in the motionless air, mixing with the sharp, tinny smell of newspaper ink.

He and associate editor J. Frank Colbert had just returned from Shreveport, where Henry Waller had boarded a train for the Louisiana State Penitentiary, accompanied by Sheriff Hutch Phillips.

They, along with several Shreveport reporters, had intercepted Sheriff Phillips and his prisoner on the platform of Shreveport's central train station. The sheriff didn't seem too surprised, although, had the train arrived on schedule, there would have been no time for interviews.

As luck would have it, the train to Baton Rouge was running late.

"Let him speak!"

A seasoned Journal reporter elbowed his way to the front of the pack.

"That would be totally up to him," Sheriff Phillips turned to his prisoner and cocked an eyebrow questioningly. "Got anything you want to say, Henry?"

"Goddamed right." Waller stopped abruptly, causing a pile-up among the reporters who had been dogging his steps.

"It's damned hard to go to jail when you are innocent of the crime charged against you and for which you for the rest of your life must remain in the pen," he said, soberly, preening at the attention he was getting and exuding a more confident air than he'd exhibited in court following his conviction.

"I was convicted falsely. Johnnie Long and those Negroes framed up on me and made me the goat."

"Gentlemen, I am as innocent of that murder as you are. But there is nothing left for me to do except to take my sentence and trust in the truth coming out later, as it's bound to do. I expect to be as good a prisoner as there is in Baton Rouge and get a commutation on my sentence, if it is possible on account of good behavior."

The whistle of the approaching train drowned out Waller's next words. Sheriff Phillips anxiously shoved his prisoner into the nearest passenger car.

Back at his office, Thomas Wafer Fuller, the peoples' conscience, could not let Waller's statement pass without comment. Sleeves rolled up, tie safely tucked between two buttons, he pounded out an editorial. He'd report the story just as it happened, of course, but the citizens had a right to know where the *Webster Signal* stood.

He was glad to know that Henry Waller intended to make a model inmate—too bad he hadn't determined to make a model citizen years ago - that would have been much better and he would not be where he was today.

Even the few people who thought he was innocent could not argue with that statement.

As to Henry Waller's claim of innocence, he supposed that was natural...guess he'd say the same thing under the same circumstances. But the truth was, Waller'd been given a fair trial before an impartial judge, with an impartial counsel. And, 12 of his countrymen, agreeable to him, had judged him guilty after listening to the evidence.

Even more convincing, Fuller thought, was that Waller himself, just this past Friday, had decided to accept the verdict rather than risk the outcome of another trial.

In the compromise settlement, engineered by Judge Sandlin, defense attorneys Barnette and Robertson agreed to withdraw the appeal of their client's verdict in exchange for the district attorney's promise not to pursue the four other capital charges - those being for the murder of Mrs. Reeves and her children.

Waller agreed to the compromise, but only after stressing to the court that his acquiescence in no way constituted an admission of guilt. Given time, he would be vindicated, he'd said. That was a smart move on his part, Fuller thought, given the bitter public sentiment against him at this point in time.

Drew also agreed to the compromise, but stipulated that, should other material or facts be uncovered, it would be sent to a grand jury. He had also taken into consideration the extraordinarily high cost of the trial, which was being estimated at $3,000 to $5,000. That's a burden he didn't want the taxpayers of Webster Parish to bear again, he told the court.

In the meantime, Fuller had learned, Drew was hoping to convince Governor Pleasant to postpone the executions of Tyson and Peters. If new information did materialize, which could be used against Waller in another trial, he'd certainly need the testimony of the two Negroes.

Others were also trying to keep the Negroes alive.

Every since Waller's sentencing, the citizens committee in Grove had been circulating petitions to have the death sentences of Tyson and Peters commuted. And they were getting a surprising response.

Judge Sandlin himself had agreed to write a letter to the Pardons Board on behalf of the condemned Negroes. "Justice must be the same for all men," he had said.

Thomas Wafer Fuller agreed with the honorable District Attorney. The Negroes should be kept alive for a time, in case new information should come to light. He personally hoped that it would.

But he was adamantly opposed to a commutation.

The Negroes didn't deserve to live.

No, indeed. Henry Waller deserved to die.

PART III

Thursday, June 28, 1917
Louisiana State Penitentiary
Angola, Louisiana

Angola, Louisiana is a small farming community situated in the extreme eastern part of the state, just a little over midways down. Folks living in Angola often count Mississippians as their closest neighbors.

This is where the main state-operated prison is located, on a former plantation where slaves once sweated and toiled over fields now worked by society's miscreants.

Since Angola lies just east of the mighty Mississippi River, the state penitentiary has the advantage of sitting right smack on top of a gently sloping, backlands alluvial plain. Thick deposits of fertile soil, deposited over hundreds of years, make the area prime for growing all kinds of crops and for grazing cattle.

With its humid, subtropical climate, Louisiana tends to be an unmerciful and sometimes deadly host during the months of June, July, and August. Whatever moisture might afford the body relief in the company of a gentle breeze sequentially becomes boiling vapor under the barrage of an unrelenting sun.

Chester Tyson had spent the past seven hours in that sun, bent over row after row of field peas, pulling them with stiff, cracked hands and placing them in huge, heavy buckets.

Sweat dripped from every pore, causing his coffee-colored skin to glisten. Every so often, a rivulet of sweat would meander down his jaw line to the southernmost tip of his chin. From there it would free-fall onto a thirsty leaf, causing him to look up with hopeful, prayerful eyes. Let it be a raindrop, he'd pray. But it never was.

After a bucket was filled, several men would empty it onto a wagon drawn by two mules. Then, the bucket would come back, empty, and Chester would look into its void and see his own future. Nothin'.

Nothin'. He'd be hanged, and then there would be nothin'. He'd come to the State pen believing in God and Jesus and Heaven and Hell. Now he knew the truth. Livin' on this earth was the Hell

153

- and since God and Jesus and Heaven wasn't in his future, death would be nothin'. It had to be nothin'. And that was all right with him.

"Tyson, boy, your ass is day-dreaming agin." A guard on horseback reined around and pointed at him with a mean-looking club he'd fashioned from a cypress knee. "Get your ass back to work."

"Yes, suh," Chester mumbled, and turned back to his picking.

A red wasp suddenly darted past his face and he slapped at it. The fields were a refuge for thousands of insects - mosquitoes, hornets, gnats, wasps - all put on earth to heap misery on mankind.

Once, not long after he arrived, he'd been weeding out between the rows when he'd heard a faint humming sound coming from the ground below his hoe. Suddenly, hell itself spewed from the bowels of the earth. It was a swarm of vengeful hornets, disturbed in their subterranean nest and bent on attaching themselves to every exposed part of his body, driving their stingers into his tender flesh and leaving behind throbbing welts.

The guards had even taken pity on him. One extracted a warm wad of chewing tobacco from his cheek, pinched off pea-sized chunks, and pressed them against each scarlet wound. The masticated potion drew out the poison and soothed the hurt.

****

Chester had refused to allow his mother, Mariah, and his new wife, Josephine, to visit him in prison. It was a long, arduous trip. And, anyway, he didn't want them to see him like this - out of control of everything from his own body odor...to his choice of living or dying.

He thought of them now as he rested his aching body in his bunk. He could feel his muscles gradually begin to relax. He'd grown used to breathing the musty, uncirculated air of the prison. But sometimes the stench of the river would permeate the thick concrete walls, and he'd bury his face in his mattress trying to find relief, only to be assailed by the offensive smell of mildew, slobber and urine.

When he mentally removed himself from his surroundings and closed his eyes against the dark, his mother and Josephine were the moving pictures behind his eyelids. He'd watch them doing their daily chores. He could hear his mother singing as she

154

hung the wash on the line, her rich voice mirroring the lost sadness of "Were You There?"

"Ohh, ohhhhh oh oh sometimes I feel I could tremble, tremble, tremble...

Were you there when they crucified my Lord?"

In his dream he would look down the road and see Josephine approaching...sashaying...her thin, flowered cotton dress showing off the curve of her full, but innocent breasts...the loose skirt undulating around her knees as she strolled. She always clutched a bundle of clothing under her arm.

More than anything in the world, Josephine wanted to be a famous seamstress. She'd started out taking on small repair jobs - sewing on buttons, patching worn sleeves and knees, adding a lace hem here or there.

"One day, Chessie," she'd say, "I'm gonna sew for all the fancy ladies...like them's that stay in town in them big ole mansions. And one of 'ems gonna like what I do so much, she's gonna invite us to live in her little guest house out back under them magnolia trees...and she won't want me to sew for nobody else."

This conversation had actually taken place about a week before Chester's life turned into pure hell. She was so young and so full of life...and hope...how could he have done this to her?

Unconsciously, Chester would fold himself into a fetal position. His throat would tighten and the sorrow and regret that was buried deep in his belly would force its way out and his whole body would jerk with silent sobs.

He couldn't cry out loud. He'd learned that the hard way. You don't do no crying to call attention to yourself.

"Heard you cryin' sweet boy," he'd heard one night shortly after his arrival. The voice was so close to his ear he could smell sour breath and sweat. Suddenly, the lower half of his body was wrenched from the bunk. He struggled helplessly as strong arms twisted his body, slamming his face into the bedding and holding it there, leaving him sprawled half on and half off the rough cot. His heart froze when someone groped the waistband of his trousers and tugged fiercely, exposing his buttocks to the faceless demons in the dark.

Whether there were two attackers...or 10...he'd never know. When the first inmate rammed his penis into Chester's exposed rear with one unmerciful thrust, the scream that tore from his lungs

155

was buried in his mattress. He knew he'd been split into, and the pain sent him reeling into a nauseous, half-faint. But there was to be no mercy. Another inmate, then another, then another...plunged again and again...pounding and pounding. With no fear of further screams, one inmate grabbed the back of Chester's head, using it for leverage to force himself deeper....and deeper...as he pounded...and pounded...

The next day, he could barely walk.

He cried quietly to himself after that.

In his favorite dream, he could touch and smell clean sheets.

He and Josephine were in their small cottage behind the big mansion in town. A breeze gently teased the curtains on the bedroom window. Dominating the room was a brass bed - devoid of all trappings save a newly-laundered stark white sheet, which enveloped the down mattress tightly. Josephine had pulled and tugged and tucked each corner, because she knew he liked it that way.

Chester's family was typically poor. But his mother had always insisted on cleanliness - it was next to Godliness, she'd said. Once a week, she'd strip every bed. Then, one-by-one, she'd dip each cotton sheet into a wooden tub of hot, soapy water and she'd work those sheets up and down 'til her fingers were raw and her arms and shoulders ached. This was a year-round ritual - it didn't matter if it was 100 degrees, or 20. Chester could remember how the steam would rise from the sheets when she lifted them and hung them on the line in the wintertime.

Oh, how he loved stretching out on those fresh, clean sheets every Sunday night...

Josephine knew he loved this, so in his dreams, their little brass bed always had clean sheets. And he loved lazily stretching his nakedness full-length across that bed. The heady, sweet perfume of magnolia blossoms filled the air. And Josephine would appear, a naked nymph whose eyes no longer shown with playful innocence, but rather womanly temptation and heat.

Crawling upon the bed, she'd caress his inner thighs lightly with the tips of her soft fingertips. In his dream within a dream, he fantasized about butterflies...When he could no longer stand it, he'd grab her shoulders and pin her back upon the pillows. She would open her legs and he'd enter her with one gentle thrust.

156

Bracing himself with his hands, his elbows straight so that his chest lightly caressed her erect nipples, he'd thrust, and then pull back...thrust, then pull back...over and over again...in and out. It drove her wild...and he loved when she'd call his name over and over again. He loved the way she said his name.

Sometimes his pent-up urges would awaken him - and he'd lay there, sweating and disoriented. As he would gradually regain his sense of surroundings, his mind would silently scream...and scream...and scream in frustration, self-pity...and terror.

Friday, June 29, 1917
Webster Parish Courthouse
Minden, Louisiana

"Let's go, John Boy."

The irritating jangle of keys signaled the approach of jailer C.J. Bell even before he called out Johnie Long's name. The jailer expertly slipped one of the keys into the door of the cell and turned.

Instead of rising, Long continued to sit on his cot, rocking gently from side to side, and looking nervous.

"Mr. Bell," he said, looking straight ahead and not at the deputy, whom he had come to like and respect, "do you think the judge'll let me say somethin' before he sentences me, huh?"

"I don't know, Johnie, he's waitin' for you now. 'Sides, what could you say that you ain't already said? What could be so important you got to say you haven't already told him?"

"I just want him to know I didn't do it," Johnie said. His eyes met Bell's, who sighed heavily.

"Now, son, you've got to quit this story-tellin'. One minute you say you was there and was witness to the killin' - next minute you wasn't anywhere near. I want to tell ya, when you pled guilty before the judge and that jury tha other day, you sealed your fate, once'd and for all."

Bell was referring to Long's "trial" on Tuesday, June 26 in the Webster Parish District Court. On Monday, the day before, Long had been prepared to denounce any earlier confessions and to fight for his freedom. His father had even acquired the law firm of Robertson, Robertson, and Johnson to handle the case.

But early Tuesday morning, Johnie once again changed his mind. His lawyers withdrew from the case and attorney W.R. Percy of the Hardy, Percy & Lee law firm was appointed by the court to represent him.

Under Louisiana law, a judge or court cannot accept a guilty plea in a capital murder case, so a jury had to be empanelled. District Attorney Harmon Drew read a written confession by Long, who then took the stand and swore before the jury that it was correct. Drew and Percy then asked the jury to find Long guilty as charged without capital punishment. They did.

"I know it won't change nothin' - but I was told pleadin' guilty was the only way to save my neck. Now, Mr. Bell, you reckon that judge is gonna stick to what that jury decided...you know, about me gettin' life like Henry got, instead of hangin?"

"'Course he will, son. The jury found you guilty without capital punishment. That means they cain't hang ya. Only peoples' gonna hang is them negras. They ain't gonna hang a nice, clean white boy like you."

But Johnie wasn't comforted.

"I just got to say it...I just got to tell it." He grew more agitated and jerked nervously.

"Let me go talk to the judge," Bell said wearily, and walked off.

When Deputy Bell returned to Johnie Long's cell about a quarter of an hour later, he was accompanied by the lawyer Percy, and two men he didn't recognize. One was introduced as a stenographer, who would record his statement; and the other as a notary, who would verify it.

A flush had appeared on Johnie's cheeks.

He ran his tongue nervously over dry lips...

And began...

****

"I was up to Mr. Reeves one day and he told me to tell Henry that if he didn't want to get into trouble about that little scrape they had, that he'd better drop it where it is. Furthermore, he said, you tell him I know things on him, otherwise, that would get him into bad trouble....

I told Henry what old man Reeves said and he said, 'That old man is a liar - he don't know nothin' on me.'

After studying a little, he said, 'That old man does know somethin' on me that could get me into trouble sure enough.'

Then Henry told me he was gonna trust me with some information. He said he heard that the old man had a lot of money, and he also knew the only way out of his trouble was to kill him.

I told him I didn't want nothin' to do with it. He said he knew some negras that hated him enough to do it for a share of the money.

He said he'd get the negras to call him out in the yard...and to use an axe so no one would be suspicious.

159

I asked Henry if he weren't afraid the negras would give him away. He said, no way, them negras would keep the secret. He said he wasn't worried about them sayin' nothin' 'cause they was too scared of him.

I told him the negras wouldn't be too scared of sayin' you put 'em up to it when they got picked up.

And that's when Henry told me he wasn't afeared of that 'cause he'd have an alibi so strong no one could prove he was there if they wanted to. He said he was going to Cotton Valley or Sarepta.

He told me not to say nothin' about it. I said it wasn't nothin' to me - I didn't want to have nothin' to do with it.

But he warned me again not to tell.

That was a little over a week before Christmas.

Then, on Christmas eve morning, Henry told me if I heard of anything being done tonight, don't let on like I know anything. He told me I didn't need to be scared, 'cause I wasn't gonna be in on it.

That's when I asked him if he was gonna have that done tonight. He said Mark and Chester told him they believed they'd rather do it Sunday night 'cause they needed the money out of it.

'They are going to do it tonight,' Henry told me. 'They said they are going to use an axe and they are going to kill the old man.'

Then I went up to my father's and went to the wedding at Ben Kirkley's and got back to my father's about 11 o'clock and went to bed and stayed all night...

....I was not present at the killin - don't even know who was - and my other statements are untrue that contradict this one. I told them because I then thought they were the only way to save my own life....As things turned out for me, they were."

****

Five minutes after signing his written renunciation, Johnie Long was facing Judge Sandlin.

Sandlin glanced briefly at the manuscript before looking at the prisoner, who stood before him with his head bowed.

"We won't waste any more of this court's time," the judge admonished. "John Jefferson Long, you are sentenced to spend the remainder of your natural life incarcerated at the Louisiana State

Penitentiary at Angola for complicity in the murder of John Nelson Reeves. I hope I never see your face again..."

Thomas Wafer Fuller's hands trembled as he ripped open the envelope.

It was postmarked Angola, Louisiana - and he could hardly wait to see what was inside.

His anticipation increased as he reverently unfolded the letter tucked within - he had recognized the writing instantly. Henry Waller's nervous scratch was unmistakable.

It was postmarked July 17, 1917.

He began to read.

"Dear Editor,

I am herein taking the liberty of dropping you this note asking space in your paper for a short contradiction of a statement made by Johnie Long which was published in the Signal some weeks ago.

It is an undisputed fact that since my arrest for the alleged murders of the Reeves family on the night of 24 of December, 1916, Johnie Long has made several statements as to the part I played in said murder.

And if the good people of Webster Parish will review these statements they will find that there are no two of them which correspond with each other.

In the last statement made by Long, he said 'I went to Henry Waller and told him that old man Reeves told me to tell him that if he (Waller) did not want to get into bad trouble that he had better let that little trouble drop where it was' and that I (Waller) said that old man Reeves does not know anything on me and I have made arrangements with Mark and Chester to kill him for a part of that money which old man Reeves has and then I will have enough to pay me out.

I want to say for the good people of Minden and Webster Parish that I, Henry Waller, have never had any such talk with Johnie Long and that he never brought me any news whatever from Mr. Reeves. Further, I want to impress on the minds of all fair-minded people that at the time of Mr. Reeves' death, he and I were on good terms and had no hard feelings of any kind toward each other.

I also wish to say that time will show to the world in general that the statements which have been so damning to me and have sent me to serve a lifetime in the pen for a crime of which I am wholly innocent, will be brought to light and to the eyes of the world in a way to make them see that Johnie Long, Mark Peters, and Chester Tyson have for some unknown reason lied in every way conceivable to bring forth the results which they have attained.

I don't know how to make the people see and believe these things I am saying, but I want them to look over the different stories told of this matter by Johnie Long and his Negro confederates and take into due consideration all the contradictory and mixed statements that they have made against me, and then weigh justice and award me my share.

It is not so hard, my being here, as it is to think that the world should think that I could commit a crime such as has been placed at my door by the people with whom I have lived among for years.

I wish to further say, although it is hard for a man to die, that the day of judgment for Mark Peters and Chester Tyson will beyond a doubt bring before the eyes of the world facts that will exonerate me of any connection with the murders of the Reeves family.

For I do not believe they will face their Maker with a lie on their souls.

As for me, my heart and conscience is entirely clear and I am living in hopes for the best, and looking forward to the time when the people of Webster Parish can see their way clear to put aside for me and place where it belongs the crime for which I am imprisoned, and let me go home to my little children and raise them in a way to wipe out the stain from their young lives which is bound to linger and cling to them throughout their whole career and mark them to the world as the children of one of the vilest of murderers; when in fact, I their father and protector am entirely innocent of any connection whatever of the crime which is laid at my door.

I have never been able at any time to bring down the sentiment of the general public to the point where they could take a general view of this matter and make them see this thing as it is.

But I want the attention of every reader of this paper to show to them that in the last statement that Long made he says that when he brought me the news Mr. Reeves sent to me that I told him 'That old man doesn't have anything on me to hurt me,' and he also says at the same time that I said to him, 'That old man does know something bad on me and I am going to tell you what I am going to do. I am going to kill him. I am not going to do it myself. I am going to have Mark and Chester do it for me.' He says also in the same conversation that I have made arrangements to have it done.

By his own statement, Long has tried to make the people believe that he brought me said news from deceased and when he told me these things he also says that I have already made arrangements to have it done.

Now the point....Taking for granted that deceased and I were on good terms, and that Long brought me this news, as he says he did, and that after considering a while as to what Mr. Reeves really did know on me to hurt me, and then that I had already made the arrangements while we were talking, Long and I. Now the question is how and when, according to Long's story, were these arrangements made?

He (Long) admits to bringing me the news and then goes on to say that I have made arrangements before getting the news. Consider then, why should a man with half a mind of his own put confidence enough in four Negroes and a white man to let them know that he was going to commit a crime of this kind? To any fair-minded reader of the paper, who would put that much confidence in anyone?

All I ask is justice, pure and simple. And I think that in a short time that the good people who read and have read the last statements which have been published against me, will be led to see the truth and come to the assistance of one who is in dire need of same."

It was signed, "Respectfully, Henry Waller, Box E, Angola, Louisiana."

William Harper bounded into his boss' office, kicking over a mile-high stack of periodicals and sending loose papers flying.

Thomas Wafer Fuller hadn't hired the ambitious young reporter because of his gracefulness. It was his ability to "sniff-out" a story that was so impressive. Judging by his actions, he had just scored.

"I just reeled in a big one, sir," William beamed, congratulating himself on his pun—"snagging" a story from DA Harmon Drew while he lunched on broiled trout at the Sanitary Cafe.

Drew wasn't known to "suffer" news reporters, but he needed a tolerant press if he was to continue a career in politics - like his father and grandfather before him.

He held his tongue, and between mouthfuls of the daily special, allowed the over-exuberant Harper to ask his questions.

Yes, he confirmed, attorney D. W. Stewart of the Webster Parish Bar had appeared before the Louisiana Board of Pardons in New Orleans the previous morning. He had presented the board a petition signed by over 600 area residents asking for the commutation of the death sentences of Chester Tyson and Mark Peters.

"Mr. Stewart and the petitioners seem to think that it would be a grave act of injustice to send the Negroes to the gallows and allow the two white men who instigated the crime to escape with life terms," Drew commented dryly, wiping tomato sauce from his mouth with a white linen napkin.

"But what do you think, sir?" Harper asked.

"I think that it is a grave act of injustice that all parties concerned are not going to the gallows - Mr. Waller and Mr. Long included. However, I must respect the finding of the jury in each case. Fine gentlemen of our parish served on those juries and, I'm sure, acted in good faith - as is their right and privilege."

Drew acknowledged that he did not personally attend the New Orleans hearing.

"But does the Pardon Board know how you feel?"

"I have written them, of course. The Governor, likewise."

"Would you be willing to share the contents of your letter?"

"Let's just say, I told them that if those two Negroes - Tyson and Peters - don't hang, I don't feel like I can ever ask a verdict of hanging in any case."

"Do you plan to pursue a second trial - to have Henry Waller or Johnie Long tried on another count of murder. There are four counts left, are there not, sir?"

"Yes, we could ask for indictments for the murder of Mrs. Reeves or any of the three children. But we don't plan to at this point. As I've said before, I think it would be a waste of the taxpayers' money and the court's time."

"Would there ever come a time that you would consider more indictments?"

"As I told the Governor, I wouldn't recommend the immediate execution of the Negroes because we might need them as witnesses should further evidence come to light to implicate Mr. Waller or Mr. Long. But that evidence would have to be very compelling. Or, if the people of Webster Parish demanded another trial, I would be remiss in my duties not to consider it."

Drew pushed back from the table and began to rise.

"But," he paused, "That doesn't seem likely. What does seem likely is that those Negroes are going to hang...It's just a shame that they will hang alone."

Harper followed him to the door.

"So you think the Pardon Board will refuse to commute the Negroes' sentences to life, sir?"

"I didn't say that," Drew said, raising his eyebrows in mock indignity.

"No, sir, but you said the Negroes would hang...and that makes me think that you think the Pardon Board will deny the request."

"Is that what you think, huh?" Drew's pace as he headed up Main towards the courthouse evinced the end of the interview, despite Harper's persistence. "I can't possibly predict what the Pardon Board will do, now can I? But if I were a betting man - and believe me son, I am not - I'd say the odds of a commutation are pretty high."

"They won't hang...."

Harper had stopped trying to pursue Drew and almost shouted the statement.

Drew didn't even look back.

"Of course they will..." he said quietly to himself.

****

Drew would have won his bet

On Monday, Oct. 22, 1917, the Louisiana Board of Pardons commuted the sentences of Chester Tyson and Mark Peters to life in prison.

The news infuriated and frustrated Thomas Wafer Fuller. Young Harper made it a point to stay out of his way that day.

"Lucky brutes," Fuller had stomped and slammed his fist on the desk, sloshing coffee and causing Harper to jump.

He vented his disappointment in the *Signal's* Friday, Oct. 26 edition.

"Hell itself would be too sweet a paradise for such brutish wretches," he wrote. "If hanging is ever justifiable, these murderers, in our judgment, should have gone to the gallows."

"The fact that the white men who were convicted of the same offense were given life sentences does not in the least mitigate the guilt of those two Negroes, or afford just grounds for a commutation of their sentence. They are just as guilty under present conditions as they would be if the white men had been hanged.

If it be right to give them only a life sentence because the white men got only a life sentence, then if the white men had been acquitted, it necessarily follows that the Negroes should also have been set free; notwithstanding their confession of guilt. This is startling, but it is nevertheless the logic of the situation.

However, it is not improbable that a large majority of the people of the parish will endorse the action of the pardoning board in commuting the Negroes' sentences, and we have no quarrel with them for doing so.

But we cannot share in the view taken by them in the matter."

Chester Tyson had spent Thanksgiving giving thanks that he was still alive.

In October, when he'd gotten word he wasn't going to hang, he'd been surprised to learn from Mr. Stewart, the attorney representing him, that white people back home were interested in saving his neck.

They had even gone so far as to put their names on a petition - that's what Mr. Stewart had called it - a petition, asking the Pardon Board to let him and Mark spend the rest of their lives in prison, rather than hang.

Chester reflected back on his first weeks in the pen - how he'd prayed for death. He missed his mama and Josephine. He closed his eyes at night terrified of being raped and beaten. The days of work in the fields were a creation of God to punish man for his sins. Yes, he had sinned in the most awful way...and he had been ready to die for it.

But as time passed, as the weeks blended into months, he missed home less. He had fewer dreams, and he was visited less at night by the sewer-mouthed rape gangs, who had gone on to more interesting, younger, sweeter prey.

Like his heart, his hands had hardened so that the field work wasn't even so bad. And the weather was cooler. Life was bearable, if not tenuous, uncomfortable, and unpredictable.

He'd begun making plans to send for his mama to visit him around Christmas. He was gonna be in here a long time - it was best that she come while she still could. He knew the trip would be hard on her - but he also realized in his heart that she would want to come at least once.

Josephine was another matter.

He didn't want her anywhere near this cesspool. She needed to get on with her life. He knew that. But seeing her would only make it harder on him.

No, Josephine could not come.

"Tyson, boy, get yer ass up, the chaplain wants to see ya." A guard suddenly appeared at Chester's cell. "Don't even ask me what it's all about, don't have no idea," he grumbled, anticipating the question.

Chester's heart had stopped. The chaplain visitin' usually meant the death of a loved one. That's the only time he came around. That, and just before someone was executed. He knew he wasn't gonna hang...so he suspected the worst.

His mama.

Chester suddenly felt helpless. He couldn't bear the thought of not seeing his mama one more time. Please, God, don't let it be my mama. Or Josephine.

The guard shuffled him into a small stark chamber bearing only a table and several hard-backed chairs. To his surprise, Mark Peters was there. He hadn't seen Mark since arriving at the pen - they'd been assigned to different blocks.

Mark looked thinner, but as brassy as ever

He nodded at Chester now as the guard motioned for him to take a seat opposite the chaplain. He turned and left.

"Mark...Chester...do you mind if we have a little prayer before we talk?"

It was a rhetorical question. The chaplain had already spread out his arms in a mock embrace and with bowed head began appealing to God for His understanding at this most difficult time and for His forgiveness of these two, who were lost but still worthy of His consideration and grace.

Chester managed a shy look up just before the chaplain issued his "Amen" to notice that Mark hadn't bowed his head, but was staring at the preacher with hard-as-flint eyes.

"I'll get right to the point, no reason to keep you fellows wondering what's going on," the chaplain said, pausing to look first at Chester, then Mark. "As you know, the Board of Pardons mercifully elected to save your necks from the gallows. They took pity on you, and because of the support of many people, they decided that you should live."

"Well, it is my sad duty to inform you that the Governor disagrees with the Pardon Board," he paused briefly to gauge the effect of his comments on the two. "Governor Pleasant has overturned the ruling of the board. He believes that you should pay the supreme penalty for your crime. I'm sorry, but he's set March 1 for your executions...I'm really very, very sorry."

Friday, April 26, 1918
Webster Parish Courthouse
Minden, Louisiana

It had been 14 months since Harmon C. Drew first swore to uphold the duties of District Attorney for Bossier and Webster Parishes. On days like today, it seemed like 14 years.

Drew sat at his desk, staring vacantly at, but not seeing, the portraits of his father and grandfather on the wall. He had just received another telegraph from Louisiana Governor Ruffin G. Pleasant in Baton Rouge, pressing him to indict Henry Waller and Johnie Long on one or more of the remaining charges in the Reeves murder case.

The governor was becoming a problem.

A real problem.

First, Gov. Pleasant had postponed the March 1 executions of Tyson and Peters, extending the length of their stay on this good earth until May 3, 1918 - over a year since their original convictions.

Now, one week shy of the hangings, Governor Pleasant was exercising his executive privilege once again and pushing the execution date to August 9.

...All this for a senseless new trial.

Pleasant just wants to ride the coattails of this highly-publicized case to advance his career after he leaves the Governor's office, Drew thought.

Well, he could leave him out of it.

He mentally conjured up a picture of himself giving his political rival the old Jack Dempsey one-two punch. Yes, he had his own agenda, and getting embroiled in another murder trial that promised no different an outcome than the first was not in the plan.

He'd endured five grand jury terms and nearly 60 jury trials since taking office in December of 1916, with not one absolute acquittal. He'd also prosecuted more bootleggers in those 14 months than had been put away in the five years previous to his becoming district attorney.

He confessed that not a day went by without his thinking of the Reeves case. No DA could have been served up a better challenge as a first case.

Oh, he knew he had done his best.

Judge Sandlin and Hutch Phillips had done their best.

In fact, he thought, had it not been for the judge and sheriff maintaining such strict order, the whole affair would have been a frightening mess. Mob law would surely have prevailed.

Feelings in the community had been running so furiously high against the accused that he had secretly feared a take-over of the jail by an angry mob. That's why Sheriff Phillips had gone to such great pains to move the prisoners so often.

It had worked. He had successfully managed to bring four Negro confederates to trial without a single incident.

And he had gotten a jury to sentence two of them to death.

But he had failed in his efforts to send the two white men to their deaths for the same crime.

Why?

Because too many people who knew next to nothing about the facts of the case had entirely too much to do with it. They had been told too much in the newspapers and had used the information to manipulate the system.

In fact, he surmised, those same people had been allowed to usurp the functions presumably belonging to the judge, the jury, and the prosecuting attorney.

These "people" had endeavored from the beginning to take the whole matter in their hands and run it.

He bet that most of the folks who signed the commutation petitions now regretted doing so. He'd had nearly a hundred...he wasn't exaggerating...a hundred people tell him so.

Damn the publicity...damn the liberal newspapers.

Publicity ruined this case, as it had many others.

He had said it before, and he would say it again - there ought to be a law against newspapers publishing facts about a case before trial.

True, he counted Thomas Fuller among his friends. But Thomas was a conservative newspaper man.

And Thomas agreed with him that the Negroes should hang.

Of course, Thomas didn't have to worry about stroking public opinion or hurting people's feelings. Take for instance the editorial he had written shortly after Governor Pleasant overturned the commutation of Tyson and Peters' sentences.

171

"One mistake should not serve as an excuse for making others," Thomas had written, applauding the Governor's actions.

Drew couldn't have said that without incurring the wrath of the men on the jury. Not that Drew feared public opinion, by damned! But he did regard and respect the people's wishes, as any good servant of the public should.

A newspaper could even speak ill of the dead, as Thomas had when he argued in print that it "was not necessary to plead anything in extenuation of the manner of living of old man Reeves."

"He might be dismissed from the situation altogether."

"But the ruthless murders of Mrs. Reeves and her children, even the baby who could have revealed nothing of the manner in which his father and mother and brothers met their deaths...would still cry out for expiation."

Yes, Thomas knew how to bend a phrase.

Was he wrong in thinking Tyson and Peters deserved to die?

He thought not. And there was no excuse for keeping them alive any longer.

Because he wasn't going to bring Waller and Long to trial again without good reason - or new facts to support the evidence. And the odds of that happening were slim.

Of course, if a majority of the people of Webster Parish pressured him to do so, he would. But that didn't appear to be happening either.

Right now, the only person pressing him was Governor Pleasant...and maybe a few others outside the parish who were ignorant of the facts.

The problem with Pleasant was that he considered himself an attorney first and a governor second. He also thought of himself as somewhat of a "local" - having been born in Shreveport and educated at Mt. Lebanon College near Minden before transferring to Louisiana State University.

For this reason, he had taken an extraordinarily keen interest in the case.

Pleasant had made a name for himself at LSU - even captained the school's first football team. But he'd gone north after graduating and studied law at Harvard and later, Yale. When he returned to Shreveport, he became city attorney.

172

In 1912, he was elected State Attorney General.

So, Drew hypothesized, the Governor just can't get trial law out of his blood.

One would think Pleasant would be too busy placating the prohibitionists and anti-vice groups while coddling the big New Orleans Democratic political machine. It also surprised him that Pleasant had kept the Negroes alive as long as he had, knowing that his political campaign was supported largely by the Ku Klux Klan, which seemed to be in the throes of a revival.

So far, the only positive thing Drew could see that Pleasant had done for Louisiana was to mobilize the war effort.

And pester him.

Well, he'd write the governor one more time expressing his opposition to a new trial. He might even suggest - should the Governor persist on a new trial - that State Attorney General Coco would be a great man to handle the prosecution...

Tuesday, August 7, 1918
Webster Parish Courthouse
Minden, Louisiana

Deputy Calhoun Garland shielded his eyes from a driving rain and hustled through the basement door of the Webster Parish Courthouse just as a violent burst of lightning exploded into the trunk of a majestic loblolly pine a few blocks north of town.

Its ferocity and closeness startled him, and he hoped the storm that had begun churning its way into town from the south at daybreak wouldn't spawn any tornadoes.

Just what they needed, he thought, tornadoes and hangin's all in the same stretch. Although, he supposed, a good rain might tend to discourage the army of newspaper reporters and nosybodies that were expected to infest the town come Thursday. Their little town of 2,000 had seemed to double in size during last year's trials.

He was still catching his breath and brushing water from the rim of his beloved Stetson when William Harper stumbled into the door, looking like a drowned rat.

Speak of the devil, Garland thought.

But he liked young Harper and usually treated him cordially...if not cautiously. After all, he was a newspaper reporter, and not to be totally trusted.

"Hey, boy, I thought you was supposed to be fightin' Germans," Garland said, remembering a *Signal* article detailing the young man's enlistment in the armed forces.

"That's right, sir, next week I'll be takin' the train to New Orleans to take my exam," he said, shaking water from his driving cap and straightening his habitually-crooked bow tie. "Then, I 'spect we'll ship out from there...I just think it's the right thing to do, you know, sir...Hope I get to see some action."

Garland listened wistfully.

Although the United States had officially entered the Great War in 1917, American soldiers had seen little action until just a few months earlier. Now the whole complexion of the war had changed, with the presence of the Americans rallying the Allies.

Garland only wished he was going in this young sprout's place. And proud to go he would be, too. Germans had some kind of nerve. But America would teach them a lesson they wouldn't soon forget.

"So you'll be around for the hangin's then?"

"Yes, sir."

"Bet that's somethin' you never thought you'd see, huh?"

"No, sir."

They walked in silence for a few seconds, each lost in his own thoughts.

"Have you ever seen someone hang?"

"Uh...not legally."

The two men had made it to the stairs, which they climbed, again falling silent, their footsteps amplified in the cavernous stairwell.

"Fact is, sir, that's what I'm here about," Harper said. They'd reached the first landing, and Garland paused to catch his breath. He wasn't as young as he used to be, and 20 years of his wife's fried chicken, milk gravy and buttered cornbread seemed to have settled around his midsection. Made it awful hard to breathe sometimes.

"I checked by the jail, and they told me the sheriff might be over here. Do you know if he's set a time yet?"

"You'll have to ask him that, he ain't told me."

"Are they going to use the jail - or will it happen so the public can witness it?"

"That's another question you'll have to ask the Sheriff. I do know that he ain't likely to release much information. You know him - he don't much cotton to nosy-bodies...or newspaper reporters. 'Course you and Mr. Fuller have always been the exception. You're local folks and you do things with respect....not like them big city fellas who come over here and show off and push their way around."

They had reached their destination, the sheriff's Tax Collection offices on the third floor.

"No disrespect to the Sheriff," Harper said quietly, leaning closer to Garland so that his voice didn't carry down the long hall. "But he might not have much to say about it. Since the law says those killers have to be executed in the parish where the crime took place, he might have to cooperate with the newspapers. But I understand what you're saying about those pushy Shreveport reporters. They think we're peons...country bumpkins, you know."

175

"Believe me, I know."

"I'm sure Mr. Fuller's gonna insist on the public having a right to know firsthand about the hangings. It's news...and the Constitution guarantees the freedom..."

Harper's voice trailed off as a shadow breached the threshold of the door they were approaching.

"Well," Garland said, slapping Harper on the back, "You're in luck, boy. Here's the Sheriff now. You can tell him all about the Constitution."

****

Sheriff Phillips had felt almost relieved when August rolled around with no word from Governor Pleasant. Apparently, Harmon Drew had convinced the governor of the foolishness of retrying Henry Waller and Johnie Long.

The sheriff admired the fiery district attorney, who he believed was as good and as fair a man as God had ever made. He knew that Drew harbored a deep disappointment over his failure to get the death sentence for Henry Waller. If there was any way he could retry the man and guarantee a different outcome, he'd not hesitate to indict him on more charges.

Sheriff Phillips knew this.

So he knew that Drew's struggle to carry out the sentences of death against Chester Tyson and Mark Peters was just his way of closing the case, and getting on with his life.

That the condemned men were Negroes was not relevant. Drew would have campaigned for their ultimate punishment had they been rich and white. He had told the sheriff on more than one occasion that his failure to win a death order for Waller did not in any way justify keeping two confessed murderers alive.

It appeared that he would finally get his wish.

Sheriff Phillips had decided that the negras should hang at first light.

Thank goodness the executions were scheduled on a weekday, and not a Saturday, or worse, a Sunday. Maybe it bein' so early, and a weekday, would keep the crowd down. He'd have to put on extra deputies for crowd control, that was for sure.

He'd decided on a public hanging, using a tree on the courthouse lawn. The tree from which they'd hang was a tough young elm that grew near the northeast corner of the courthouse, separated from the jail by Back Street and a parking lot. From their

176

window in a cell on the second floor of the jail, Chester Tyson and Mark Peters could watch as preparations for their deaths were made.

The condemned men had been quartered in the jail since a few days before their last scheduled execution date, when the sheriff had traveled to Baton Rouge personally to pick them up and escort them back to town.

But, Governor Pleasant had postponed the hangings once again.

He almost felt sorry for the two negras...almost.

First, they're sentenced to hang, then the Pardon Board says they don't have to hang, then the Governor says they do have to hang, then the postponements - this thing had been goin' on for two years now...

It was time for closure...

The victims deserved it.

The court officials deserved it.

Yes, even he deserved it.

He'd been busy enough trying to rid the parish of bootleggers and moonshiners.

Three months earlier, devastation had hit the town in the form of a fire of mysterious origins that leveled the Minden Lumber Company and the Minden Electric Light & Power Company. Luckily there were no deaths or serious injuries, but nearly 300 people had lost their jobs.

Yes, it had already been a hard summer.

And now, because of a new law, he had this hangin' thing thrown right back into his own backyard - and he didn't like it. Why couldn't they just take care of executions at the State pen, like in the past? But Governor Pleasant and the Legislature argued that a killer should be executed in the same jurisdiction of the crime because victims' families and concerned citizens had a right to attend—and because it would serve as a bigger deterrent to crime. He didn't know if he agreed with that, but he was sworn to uphold the law.

And he had every intention of doing just that.

They had complained and said criminals didn't deserve such luxury, but the taxpayers of Webster Parish had coughed up $16,000 in 1906 to build a modern, multi-level jail.

This was just two years after the completion and occupancy of a new $45,000 courthouse that rivaled any other in north Louisiana for its graceful, domed architectural style and marbled hallways.

Sheriff Phillips was thankful for both of them. Since the Sheriff's Tax Collection Offices were located in the courthouse, folks needing to call at his office with tax business didn't have to suffer visiting the jail.

All around him, the sheriff could see signs of progress

The curbing and guttering of Main Street had been finished, and workmen were now undertaking the tedious job of laying red clay bricks end-to-end and side by side the entire length of the business boulevard, from Chaffe's Drug Store on the corner of Pine Street to Will Fuller's Garage on the northeast end of downtown.

Sheriff Phillips had gladly agreed to allow minor violators to pay off their jail fines by working on the streets. Some of his trustees were also helping out. After the curbs were poured, his men had shoveled gravel onto the roadbed in preparation for the bricks. His philosophy was, keep a prisoner busy and you keep him out of trouble. Keep him physically worn out and he behaves even better.

In Sheriff Phillips' opinion, the street work was long overdue. Dust in summer and mud in spring were bad enough under the churning trudge of horses, buggies, and wagons. But automobiles had pushed the downtown merchants, shoppers, and civic leaders to the point of intolerance.

Minden's Board of Aldermen had finally given in to public pressure and ordered the work.

Now, with an improved and modern road surface, it would be up to City Marshall J. F. Maddry to keep the jitney operators and fearless young cads from speeding and running over unsuspecting pedestrians. Both were already notorious for exceeding the 8 mph speed limit.

This morning, however, Sheriff Phillips would gladly have traded places with Marshall Maddry.

It was only 4 a.m. and already his olfactory senses were being assaulted by the heady aroma of country cured bacon frying in a skillet alongside fresh eggs, red potatoes, bell peppers, and green onions. He could picture the huge cathead biscuits his trustee cook would place alongside a healthy serving of grits drowning in butter.

Normally, the smells emanating from the jail kitchen would perk his appetite. But in the seasonably warm, pre-dawn hours of this day, they were a depressing reminder.

This would be Chester Tyson and Mark Peters' last meal.

Though the sparsely spaced gaslights afforded the sheriff a limited view of the courthouse grounds from his office in the jail, it didn't appear that a crowd had begun to gather. The hangings were set for six - people probably wouldn't start showing up until five.

All was quiet in the jail. It had been that way for several days—the other prisoners being solemn and reflective, the deputies and jailers jumpy and nervous.

Since the prisoners would have to be marched from the jail across Back Street and through the parking lot of the courthouse to be hanged, Sheriff Phillips had summoned all of his deputies to be on hand. Every deputy from every shift would be present to keep the peace. At Judge Sandlin's suggestion, he had also sworn in a dozen special deputies.

Right now the condemned men were in their cells meeting with Reverend J.R. Moore, pastor of the Mt. Calm Missionary Baptist Church. The reverend was doing most of the talking. Chester and Mark just listened, eating their hearty breakfasts as if there was a tomorrow.

Mark had decided early on that if he was to die, he wouldn't let anyone know how afraid he was. And deep down, he was terrified. Sometimes he regretted talking bad about God, and secretly he prayed to Him. Mostly he prayed that he wouldn't break down and act like a coward when the noose was put around his neck. Sometimes he prayed that it wouldn't hurt. Sometimes he prayed that God wouldn't send him into a fiery hell occupied by putrid evil spirits.

179

Chester, though the weaker man by nature, appeared the most calm. He had questioned God's omnipotence and the existence of Heaven when he first arrived at Angola. But his religious roots had been too deep. His mama had taught him well...had set a wonderful example. In fact, he worried more about her and Josephine than he did about himself.

As he ate his breakfast, half listening to the right Reverend Moore, he wished that there was some way his mother and Josephine could be spared seeing him hang. But he knew they would be there. And he was more ashamed than frightened.

****

An intuitive man by nature, Hutch Phillips hadn't been able to shake an uneasy feeling for several days. This was probably the reason his men were acting on edge this morning. His own nerves were frayed, and they sensed it.

At 5:30, he ordered Deputy Garland to place a call to the Governor's Office.

"I feel sure the Governor will want to know that everything is progressing according to plan," Phillips told Garland. "Even at this hour, someone in the Mansion should be awake."

He walked off, motioning for two deputies to follow. They would handle the horses, upon whose backs the condemned men would sit. No use in building a gallows - it was a senseless waste of time and money. It might be another 100 years before they were used again.

Outside, a crowd had begun to gather.

He motioned for several more deputies and ordered them to clear out an area around the tree, and to stay put to insure that no one got trampled by a horse or threw rotting vegetables.

Although time had diminished the degree of disgust and hatred some citizens felt towards the killers, their animosity was still a palpable thing. And, after a dormant period, the Ku Klux Klan seemed to be enjoying a revival. He feared their infiltration into the crowd more than anything else.

Right now, the jail was teaming with deputies and sworn volunteers waiting for orders. The sheriff obliged.

"I want you two to bring the wagon around and back it up fairly close to the tree," the sheriff instructed. "We'll use it to stand on - then we can use it to bring the bodies back here....Go on, I want you to do that right now."

180

He hailed several more deputies.

"I want you four to bring down Tyson and Peters," he said, pointing to each man. "Be sure they're handcuffed - you don't have to shackle 'em. I want two of you men with them at all times - one on each side. Watch at the door, and when I give you the word, bring 'em on out. Don't hesitate...don't stop...bring them straight out."

"Now, I want you fellas to form a kind of line from the jail door to the tree," he said, signaling another group of men. "It'll probably take about eight of you...just be sure no one interferes with our prisoners. We don't want a spectacle...we want this to be as civilized as possible. Do you all understand that?"

"Yes, sir..."

"You got it, Sheriff...."

Everyone signaled they understood.

Sheriff Phillips removed his hat and mopped sweat from his forehead and neck.

"Let's everyone get to their places then."

****

Ten minutes later, he was hoisting himself gingerly onto the bed of the wagon that would serve as stage and podium for the hanging "ceremony."

The wagon had been used in so many whiskey raids that its boards reeked of sour mash. It would go up like kindling if anyone struck a match too near it.

The sun would soon begin its slow ascent from behind the wooded Driskill hills east of Minden into the dry, hot August sky. In another hour, he would have to squint to see.

But this grim task wouldn't take an hour.

From his vantage point he could see most of the crowd. Considering the hour, it was pretty large. He estimated 100 or so. Many faces were familiar. There were a few Negroes - he recognized Mariah Tyson. She was standing, silently weeping, beside a young girl who must have been Chester's wife. The young girl was holding on to Mrs. Tyson and crying bitterly.

If the other Negroes in the crowd had close ties to the condemned men, he couldn't tell.

To his relief, everyone else seemed calm.

He had asked two area ministers to participate in the executions. Rev. Moore and Rev. A.J. Brown of the Mt. Zion

CME Church would pray for the men after they were declared dead. He had the local Negro funeral home director standing by to receive the bodies.

Harmon Drew was there in an official capacity, representing the State. Standing next to him were Thomas Wafer Fuller and William Harper. Reporters from the *Shreveport Times* and *Shreveport Journal* were there, as were others he didn't recognize.

He wondered what these people expected to see. How could they even begin to imagine how horrible it was to watch someone die? He would bet most of them had never even seen a lifeless body – much less an actual death. Did they know how the sight of these men dying would be forever fused into their memories? This wasn't some Wild West sideshow at the parish fair...bang, bang...an actor falls to the ground, feigning a glorious death.

In the months to come, it would not matter that these two men had participated in a cold, gruesome crime. It would not matter because what they would recall would be two helpless men, hands tied behind their backs, tow sacks covering their heads, jerking and gagging at the end of a rope. Jerking and jerking...and then suddenly still. They would smell them. Urine and feces. That's what they would remember.

These people had not seen the bloody bodies...the innocent young bodies – butchered while these men stood by and did nothing.

They would not, could not, remember that.

Sheriff Phillips remembered that – and still he would not choose to stand here and watch these men die. But he had no choice.

Suddenly, he felt tired. And he was developing one of those "sick" headaches. He was ready for this story to end.

He motioned for one of his deputies to pass the word along for his men to bring out the prisoners.

When they appeared at the door to the jail and began their slow approach toward the two ropes waiting for them, Mariah Tyson began to wail. It was a heart-breaking keen that touched even the hardest heart and doused the grousing crowd into an uncomfortable silence.

Chester sobbed and dropped his head. He couldn't look at his mother. His heart was breaking.

Mark stared straight ahead.

They stumbled forward toward the makeshift gallows.

When they had almost reached the wagon, Sheriff Phillips noticed Calhoun Garland waving at him from the doorway of the jail.

"What in blazes could Garland want," he thought to himself, his earlier uneasiness returning.

One of his deputies managed to get close enough to whisper without the entire crowd overhearing.

"Garland says he finally got the Governor on the telephone. He wants to talk to you."

Phillips quickly rattled off instructions for his deputies to guard the two prisoners. He half-ran to the jail, where Garland was standing holding the phone.

"This is Sheriff Phillips," he said, taking the phone from his deputy's hand.

"Yes, Sheriff Phillips, I'm certainly glad you called. The telegraph lines have been down because of the storm on Tuesday. I had wired you, but obviously you didn't get the message. I'm staying the execution. I've decided to handle the case myself - to retry Henry Waller and Johnie Long for murder with capital punishment. I will ask Mr. Drew to assist me."

Sheriff Phillips was stunned into silence.

"Sheriff? Are you still on the line?"

"I'll pass that word along to Mr. Drew," he said, finally regaining his composure.

He returned the phone to its cradle and noticed his hands were trembling. He turned, and sat down.

"Sweet Jesus," Hutch Phillips sighed, resting his bowed head in his hands. Had it not been for his intuition and a call to the Governor's Office, Chester Tyson and Mark Peters would both be dangling from the end of a rope.

Saturday, July 10, 1920
State Capitol Building
Baton Rouge, Louisiana

John M. Parker was a shrewd businessman, an avid outdoorsman, and a conservative, yet progressive leader.

When, in May of 1920, he succeeded Ruffin G. Pleasant as Governor of the State of Louisiana, he inherited a whole host of problems, not the least being a criminal case that had been ongoing since December of 1916.

Though born into the family of a wealthy cotton farmer and merchant, Parker knew and appreciated hard work. He'd inherited much of his family's properties in the Mississippi Delta, which he sold in 1912 to devote full time to commercial cotton trading.

And he was good at it. He became the youngest president of both the Cotton Exchange and the New Orleans Board of Trade.

He was *very* good at it.

And, he was very wealthy.

He was also very opinionated.

Being a businessman, he tended to side with anti-labor forces, and therefore became a bitter enemy of the New Orleans "political machine." That was okay by him - he detested career politicians anyway, especially those Democratic puppets of the big city bosses.

He also hated the Ku Klux Klan. He didn't totally disagree with their political views, but abhorred their methods - such as hiding behind masks and playing on people's fears. Besides, his wife was Catholic. And Catholics were on the KKK's hate list - along with Jews and niggers.

So his dislike for Labor, his unwillingness to play "machine" politics, and his condemnation of the KKK had worked against him in 1916 when he made his first bid for Governor of Louisiana on the Progressive ticket. Although he polled 38 percent of the vote, he lost to Pleasant - or "Unpleasant," as he had nicknamed his opponent.

It was a bitter pill, because what he liked most was honesty and efficiency in a government that was run like a business - not one run by powerful Labor leaders and white supremacists.

John Parker had always wanted to think that Theodore Roosevelt was attracted to him for these very traits - his business acumen, his honesty, and his penchant for reform politics.

In truth, Parker later realized, it was his love of hunting and fishing, and his ability to treat Roosevelt to "bully" exciting hunting and fishing excursions that probably played a larger role in the friendship.

Anyway, when John Parker decided to join the Progressive Party, he had been proud to stand shoulder-to-shoulder alongside Teddy Roosevelt as they launched their "New Nationalism" platform. That was between 1912 and his gubernatorial loss in 1916.

Coming off that loss, Parker was ecstatic when the National Progressive Party nominated Teddy for President of the United States - with him as his running mate.

Only problem for Parker - Roosevelt turned the nomination down, electing to support Republican candidate Charles Evans Hughes against incumbent President Woodrow Wilson, a Democrat.

Thus ended the friendship of Teddy Roosevelt and John Milliken Parker.

Parker campaigned for Wilson.

Wilson won re-election.

And now, four years later, Parker was in the Louisiana Governor's Mansion, having campaigned and won on promises of increased revenue for education and roads, the need for a new state constitution, the end of machine rule, and cheaper fuel for the inhabitants of New Orleans and all of Louisiana.

But the KKK was still thwarting him. And the KKK was a strong force to be reckoned with in Louisiana politics - as his closest aide, Joseph Terrebonne, had just reminded him.

He was sitting at his desk, poring over four years worth of papers and projects his predecessor had, for one reason or another, ignored, refused to consider, or elected not to touch.

It was obvious why Pleasant had passed over some of the demands, appeals, and requests for favors. They were either unimportant, too drastic, or too politically "hot" to handle.

So they were now Parker's problem.

"Why should I have to worry about the damned KKK now?" Governor Parker leaned back in his chair, locked his fingers behind his neck, closed his eyes and sighed deeply.

"Because, sir, you have a great many things you want to accomplish over the next four years. And directly, or indirectly, the KKK can make your job easy - or, to put it bluntly, they can make it hell," Terrebonne answered.

"Why can't people see the truth for the truth?" Parker sat up abruptly and slapped the top of the desk. "Damn right I despise the KKK. I don't like the way they operate. They're yellow and gutless. Instead of using the political process, they have to hide behind masks and burn crosses - terrifying innocent people and getting a bad name for every Southerner. The organization is a useless pile of dog crap."

"There are many people who don't agree with you, sir," Terrebonne countered, playing the devil's advocate. It was a game he and his boss played often.

"The KKK ought to be able to figure out where I'm coming from without too much intelligence. Why do they think I could not support the 19th Amendment. Hell, I believe women are entitled to take part in government. I would never deny a daughter of mine anything that I would give to my son. But when you allow uninformed people to vote - to begin manipulating the system of law and order, you're going to have chaos. We need educated, informed voters. Hell, most men don't deserve the right to vote. It's a privilege they squander."

Terrebonne raised his eyebrows, but did not comment.

"You know it all started with the Brits," Parker reflected, unconsciously tapping his fingers on the desk and regressing on the Women's Suffrage issue. "But you see, they recognized the need for an education - so they stipulated that a woman has to be over the age of 30 to vote. Not us Americans, noooooo. We just say, 'Come on, everybody vote!' Like it doesn't matter a damn about qualifications."

Parker sneaked a grinning peak at Terrebonne.

"Yeah, I know, I'm on my soapbox," he said.

Terrebonne still did not respond.

"Too bad politicians can't say what the people need to hear."

186

He finally hit a nerve with his aide.

"Well, the fact is, sir, the KKK and most people probably aren't smart enough to figure you out."

Parker grinned.

"Got that right."

Both men became quiet.

"So what do we do about this?" Governor Parker broke the spell, balancing a document in each of his open palms as if weighing them.

"On the one hand, we've got this official-looking paper from the Board of Pardons - signed by, um, looks like over 600 people - that says two Webster Parish Negroes who were convicted of murder - in 1917 no less - and sentenced to hang...were not the primary perpetrators of the crime. That, in fact, two white men planned and carried out the crime. But - and this is a big BUT - the white men were both found guilty and sentenced only to life in prison."

Terrebonne was well aware of the two papers. He knew that the case should have been brought to an end years ago by Governor Pleasant. He secretly suspected that Pleasant was too afraid of the consequences either way to make a final decision.

He had researched the matter at Governor Parker's request, and learned about Governor Pleasant's overturning the Pardons Board decision to commute the Negroes' sentences.

Pleasant had then begun a two-year game of assigning and delaying execution dates. His last formal postponement had been made in August of 1918, just hours before the two men were to hang.

Then, oddly, he had ignored the case altogether until two months ago, when he had ordered the Bossier-Webster District Court to set June trial dates for the two white men.

They would be tried on additional murder charges stemming from the same case. Pleasant would handle the prosecution himself, and had ordered Bossier-Webster District Attorney Harmon C. Drew to assist. Being the top prosecutor in the criminal district court, Drew could not very well decline.

It had become all too crystal clear to Terrebonne and Governor Parker that Pleasant's desire to try the case was a malicious attempt to "show up" Harmon Drew. Since Drew had failed to get death sentences for two convicted murderers - Parker would just show him how.

What exactly motivated Pleasant toward this end, neither Terrebonne nor John Parker knew. But Drew was a potentially powerful man, and Pleasant was not without further political ambitions. Pleasant probably wanted the upper hand if Drew was to aspire politically in his own "backyard."

Governor Parker remained poised with the papers in each hand, looking at his aide questioningly.

The other document was a death warrant.

The Governor could, with a flourish of his pen and Drew's blessings, assign an execution date to the two Negroes.

He would satisfy Drew.

And, he would win a margin of respect from the KKK.

On the other hand, Judge John N. Sandlin, who handled the case, appeared to be an overwhelming favorite for election to Congress in September. He would, no doubt, enjoy favor in Washington political circles and would be positioned to bring much good to the State of Louisiana.

Among the papers in the case file was a letter from Judge Sandlin encouraging a commutation of the Negro's sentences to life in prison.

Governor Parked dropped his hands, as if the weight of the papers had become too much to bear.

"Is this a race problem...or a political problem?" he said, almost to himself. "Why did my predecessor refuse to act on this? What's right? Come on, help me out here, Terrebonne. Don't just sit there enjoyin' seeing me squirming in anguish."

"It believe it's a problem for your own conscience, sir," Terrebonne commented dryly.

"Well tell me somethin' I don't know. Do they deserve to die or not? Would they deserve to die if they were White men...no, better yet, would they deserve to live if they were White men? I would like to think that we are not so eaten up by bigotry here in Louisiana that we would send a Negro to his death simply because he is a Negro."

"Well, now Governor, if we were so prejudiced, we wouldn't be having this problem or this conversation. Those people in Webster Parish would not have asked the Pardon Board to commute the sentences of these two men...and they probably would have hanged by now."

"And," Terrebonne was on a roll, "for some people, right and wrong just downright transcends color."

"Yeah, that's for some people. I'd like to think I was one of those people."

"You know, Governor, bigots live everywhere. You can't pick up a newspaper without readin' some story about people being mistreated somewhere. Look at the hard time the Irish and Polish are having in the northeast. And you know personally that Catholics aren't welcome everywhere, much less Jews. We're probably more tolerant of them here than anywhere else. Bigots aren't exclusive to the South...They've got just as many in Boston, and New York, and Chicago."

"But that's the trouble, don't you see? I don't even know if this **is** a racial question. Will it be perceived more as a 'Crime and Punishment' issue? Do these men deserve to die? Is what they did pardonable just because someone else involved in the whole affair got off with a lighter sentence?"

"I'm just glad it's you having to make that decision, Governor."

"And for that sentiment, I'm payin' you good money."

Governor Parker sighed.

Slowly and deliberately, he placed both documents before him.

He stared at one, then the other. One, then the other.

Finally, he reached out and took a quill pen from its resting place on the massive mohagony desk used by a generation of Louisiana governors.

Carefully, he dipped the pointed silver tip of the pen into a small bottle of midnight black ink.

He pulled one of the papers forward.

And he signed his name.

EPILOGUE

June 22, 1922
Louisiana State Penitentiary
Angola, Louisiana

Johnie Long heaved all 160 pounds of his lanky frame into first pushing, then pulling a heavy, smelly barrel of garbage through the doorway of the prison mess hall.

The blast of June heat that assaulted him once outside barely registered - after all, it wasn't unusual for the temperature in the kitchen where he worked to register in excess of 100 degrees during the summer.

He squinted into the broiling sun, wiping away a droplet of sweat that had wandered onto his eyelid.

Johnie had spent two of the past five years at the Louisiana State Penitentiary working as a cook's helper.

He had been a model prisoner, and now he was a trustee.

Being a trustee meant that one could enjoy a little more freedom where freedom was coveted, could spend a little more time in the library, or doing odd jobs for the warden or prison staff...could have a little bit bigger helpin's at mealtime, and might even be allowed a treat every now and again.

It meant that he could, without supervision, maneuver a barrel of stinking garbage out the rear door of the mess hall. Most prisoners saw the outside only during their daily hour of exercise in the yard.

Johnie had just turned to go back inside when a wagon pulled by two mules approached. He recognized the driver, one of the guards, and waved.

"Hey, hold up there," the guard hollered, signaling for Johnie to stop. "At boy who usually helps me load this stuff woke up with the craps this mornin' - come on and help me get these barrels on the wagon."

Johnie obliged, glad to remain outside for a few minutes longer.

"Okay, hop on. I can't very well unload the shit myself."

Grinning, Johnie leaped up onto the seat next to the guard, who clucked his tongue and flicked the reins, signaling his mules to move.

The wagon and its load headed off down the dirt drive at a snail's pace. Nothin' moved fast in Louisiana in June. 'Cept the flies, of course, which hovered around the garbage barrels, lighting on Johnie's face and ears and arms in the irritating manner flies master at an early age.

The stench of pigs soon assailed Johnie's senses, and he realized they were taking their barrels of treasure to the prison's swine operation. He'd gotten used to a lot of foul smells since first arriving at the state pen five years earlier, but the acrid, sour smell of swine wallowing in fetid garbage and their own feces still bothered him.

Since the pig farm constituted a sizely financial enterprise for the State prison, with the fattest swine being hauled off to town for auctioning, the operation was conveniently located adjacent to the prison's main access road, which, in turn, led directly to the State highway.

Johnie felt excited at being so far away from his small concrete world.

The guard maneuvered the mules and his load onto an elevated wooden platform that fell off into a three-foot deep trough where 40 to 45 pigs waited - snorting, squealing, and climbing over each other in anticipation.

"Okay, boy, let's get unloaded. Bring me that flat of plywood, lean it against the back of the wagon and we'll just slide those babies right on down."

He directed as they worked.

When the barrels were all unloaded, they slid them one-by-one to the end of the plank walkway. Down below, the pigs waited none-too-patiently.

"Okay, boy. Grab you a shovel and start slinging."

With that, both men commenced shoveling the garbage and flinging it into the midst of the hungry, ill-mannered swine.

"God damn it!" The guard drew up suddenly, swearing, and grabbing at his wrist.

"God damn...must a slung my watch off into that shit. I can't lose that watch - my boy brought it back from the War - took it off one of them Germans. He'd have a fit if he knowed I lost it."

As Johnie watched, the guard sat, turned and then side-stepped cautiously into the sunken pen. The pigs, still hungry, refused to budge as he worked among them, keeping his back to

Johnie, concentrating on the slimy ground, cursing at every opportunity.

It was about that time that Johnie felt a sudden urge to relieve himself.

He said as much to the distracted guard.

"Yeah, just go on over there behind the barn - ain't nobody around that's gonna see you," the guard instructed, turning back to his search.

Johnie walked off.

He stood relieving himself, staring across a junkyard of rusting barrels, discarded appliances, tall weeds, and old farm implements...a junkyard leading to the road.

Suddenly he was walking toward that road.

He paused...and glanced back.

The guard continued his search, his back still to the prisoner.

He reached a barbed wire fence.

Only slightly hesitating, he squeezed himself through the upper and lower strands.

He was on the road.

He looked both ways. Once more he looked back.

Nothing. No one.

He crossed the road, and headed toward what appeared to be a path meandering into a dense thicket of trees.

One more quick look back.

And he was gone.

Judge John N. Sandlin became one of Louisiana's most beloved United States Congressmen. In the mid-thirties, he became a close confidant of Franklin D. Roosevelt, who persuaded him to run against powerful U.S. Senator Huey Long. However, before the election could take place, Long was assassinated. The pro-Long forces, perpetuating a non-fact-based accusation that Sandlin was somehow involved in the assassination plot, won the election. Judge Sandlin is buried in the historical Minden Cemetery. His grave marker reads, "To Know Him Was to Love Him."

Like his father before him, District Attorney Harmon C. Drew became a District Judge for the 2nd (later the 26th) Judicial District of Louisiana, as did his son, and his grandson, after him.

Sheriff Hutchinson Phillips, elected to his first term in 1916, would win re-election to the post two more times, retiring in 1928, but continuing to work in law enforcement as a deputy.

Anderson Heard was 25 years old when he became incarcerated at the Louisiana State Penitentiary. He worked as a cane cutter and was apparently a model prisoner, earning "good time" and winning his release from prison on August 21, 1927.

Larkin Stewart, 23, contracted pneumonia and influenza, and died on November 8, 1918 - less than two years after arriving at the Louisiana State Penitentiary.

Johnie Long escaped from the Louisiana State Penitentiary on June 22, 1922 at the age of 26. He was never recaptured.

On July 10, 1920, Louisiana Governor John M. Parker commuted the death sentences of Chester Tyson and Mark Peters to life in prison. They were both discharged from the Louisiana State Penitentiary on April 18, 1936 after spending nearly 20 years in prison.

Henry M. Waller was 34 years old when he entered the Louisiana State Penitentiary on March 27, 1917. He died of tuberculosis on December 5, 1926 at the age of 43. He is buried on the grounds of the state prison at Angola. He maintained his innocence to his death.

Cody Reeves drowned in Bayou Dorcheat less than two years after the murder of his entire family.